THE RUSSIAN URBAN SUSTAINABILITY PUZZLE

THE RUSSIAN URBAN SUSTAINABILITY PUZZLE

How Can Russian Cities Be Green?

POLINA ERMOLAEVA
Kazan Federal University, Russia

YULIA ERMOLAEVA
Federal Research Center for Sociology Russian Academy of Sciences, Russia

OLGA BASHEVA
Federal Research Center for Sociology Russian Academy of Sciences, Russia

IRINA KUZNETSOVA
University of Birmingham, UK

VALERYA KORUNOVA
Center of Advanced Economic Research at the Academy of Sciences of the Republic of Tatarstan, Russia

emerald PUBLISHING

United Kingdom – North America – Japan – India
Malaysia – China

Emerald Publishing Limited
Howard House, Wagon Lane, Bingley BD16 1WA, UK

First edition 2021

Reprints and permissions service
Contact: permissions@emeraldinsight.com

British Library Cataloguing in Publication Data
A catalogue record for this book is available from the British Library

ISBN: 978-1-83982-631-3 (Print)
ISBN: 978-1-83982-630-6 (Online)
ISBN: 978-1-83982-632-0 (Epub)

Printed and bound by CPI Group (UK) Ltd, Croydon, CR0 4YY

ISOQAR
REGISTERED
Certificate Number 1985
ISO 14001

ISOQAR certified Management System, awarded to Emerald for adherence to Environmental standard ISO 14001:2004.

INVESTOR IN PEOPLE

CONTENTS

List of Figures vii
About the Contributors ix
List of Contributors xi
Acknowledgments xiii

Introduction 1
P. Ermolaeva

1. Russian Sustainable Cities: "Putting the Puzzle Together" 5
P. Ermolaeva, V. Korunova, O. Basheva and Y. Ermolaeva

2. Puzzle 1: Air and Water Quality 19
I. Kuznetsova and V. Korunova

3. Puzzle 2: Sustainable Transport and Mobility 31
P. Ermolaeva

4. Puzzle 3: Energy Efficiency and Energy Consumption 43
Y. Ermolaeva

5. Puzzle 4: Waste Management 57
Y. Ermolaeva and P. Ermolaeva

6. Puzzle 5: Green and Blue Zones 71
O. Basheva and I. Kuznetsova

7. Puzzle 6: Environmental Governance and Politics 83
O. Basheva, V. Korunova and I. Kuznetsova

Conclusion 97
P. Ermolaeva, Y. Ermolaeva, O. Basheva, I. Kuznetsova and V. Korunova

References 107
Index 131

LIST OF FIGURES

Figure 2.1.	Practices of Citizens to Minimize the Negative Impact of Air Pollution (%).	23
Figure 2.2.	Practices of Citizens to Clean the Tap Water (%).	25
Figure 3.1.	Citizens' Assessments of Different Features of the Transport System in Russian Megacities (Average Points, Where "5" – Excellent, "3" – Moderate, and "1" – Not Satisfactory).	38
Figure 3.2.	The Main Reasons for Not Using a Bike/Scooter (%).	41
Figure 4.1.	Energy-saving Practices (%).	54
Figure 4.2.	Water-saving Practices (%).	55
Figure 5.1.	Experts' Scheme of Zero-waste Management in Russia.	65
Figure 5.2.	Household Waste Management Practices (%).	67
Figure 6.1.	Do You Walk in Parks/Squares and Outdoor Recreation Areas in Your City? (%).	77
Figure 7.1.	In Your Opinion, Are Local Authorities Actively Involving the Population in Environmental Decision-making? (%).	92
Figure 7.2.	The Most Urgent Environmental Conflicts Stated by the Population (%).	94

ABOUT THE CONTRIBUTORS

Dr Olga Basheva is Research Fellow at Kazan Federal University and the Federal Center of Theoretical and Applied Sociology of the Russian Academy of Sciences. Research interests include: environmental sociology, socio-ecological rehabilitation processes, collective actions, networks of nongovernmental organizations and social movements, social capital, volunteering, media research, social networks, and media. Since 2007, she has participated in more than 10 Russian research projects. In 2019, Olga became the head of the research project "Emergency volunteering as a reply to the natural and technological challenges in Russia."

Dr Polina Ermolaeva is Associate Professor at the Department of Sociology of Kazan Federal University, Research Fellow at the Federal Center of Theoretical and Applied Sociology of the Russian Academy of Sciences and the Center of Advanced Economic Research. Her research interests center on sustainability transitions, climate research, environmental governance, sustainable cities, and volunteering in emergency. Polina led over 50 global projects for such organizations as UBER, the World Bank Foundation, Open Society Foundation, British Petroleum, Fulbright, IREX, Russian Scientific Foundation, and others.

Yulia Ermolaeva is Research Fellow at Kazan Federal University and the Federal Center of Theoretical and Applied Sociology of the Russian Academy of Sciences, Secretary and Organizer of events at the Russian Society of Sociologists. Her area of professional interests include the interdisciplinary studies in the field of environmental sociology, sociology of professions, waste management, renewable energy sources, sustainable production and consumption, and ecoactivism. Yulia took part in more than 10 research projects on the study of engineering professions and dynasties, the problems of green cities, waste management, the critical state of natural and social systems, and ecoactivism.

Valerya Korunova is Research Fellow at Kazan Federal University and the Center of Advanced Economic Research at the Academy of Sciences of the Republic of Tatarstan. Research interests include the analysis of environmental awareness and ecological culture of youth, ecological communication, the content and features of the (re)translation of ecological information in mass media, urban environmental risks, and their awareness of the citizens.

Dr Irina Kuznetsova is Research Fellow and Lecturer at the School of Geography, Earth and Environmental Sciences of the University of Birmingham, UK. Her recent projects focused on population displacement from Ukraine and funded by AHRC, British Academy, and Wellcome trust. She is also a coinvestigator in Horizon 2020 project on the impact of migration on rural communities. Irina works also on migration from Central Asia in Russia. Recently, she started studies on mental health and forced displacement in Nigeria, Brazil, and Japan.

LIST OF CONTRIBUTORS

Olga Basheva	Federal Research Center for Sociology Russian Academy of Sciences, Russia
Polina Ermolaeva	Kazan Federal University, Russia
Yulia Ermolaeva	Federal Research Center for Sociology Russian Academy of Sciences, Russia
Valerya Korunova	Center of Advanced Economic Research at the Academy of Sciences of the Republic of Tatarstan, Russia
Irina Kuznetsova	University of Birmingham, UK

ACKNOWLEDGMENTS

This work was supported by the Russian Science Foundation under grant number: 17-78-20106 "Russian cites in the context of new social and environmental challenges: building complex interdisciplinary model of an assessment of 'green' cities and strategies for their development in Russia."

INTRODUCTION

P. Ermolaeva

Nowadays Russian cities are facing a wide range of socio-economic, environmental, and technological risks. Many of them have taken several decades to develop, including severe air and water pollution, the "double transition" process (Yanitsky, 2018b), the redistribution of private property, changes in geopolitical situations, and the energy crisis. On a micro level, retrospective analysis shows the reinforcement of old social and environmental risks and the appearance of new ones; these include the waste crisis, air pollution, environmental injustice, citizens' low ownership of urban and environmental policymaking, and environmental conflicts. At the same time, further positive developments have been observed in cities' green infrastructure, public transport, rapid digitalization, a tendency toward the routinization of environmental values, and at a much lower degree, environmental practices.

There have been studies on these processes individually, such as the analysis of sustainability development goals for Russia (Bobylev & Solovyeva, 2017; Gurieva & Dzhioev, 2016), waste issues and practices in Russian cities (Y. Ermolaeva, 2018, 2019b), climate change (Dronin & Kirilenko, 2011; Richler, 2019), environmental activism and grassroots (Henry, 2010; Yanitsky, 2012, 2018c), Russian environmental politics (P. Ermolaeva, 2014; Korppoo, Tynkkynen, & Hønneland, 2015), and digitalization of Russian cities (Boykova, Ilina, & Salazkin, 2016); however, holistic studies of Russian cities' sustainability are very poorly investigated and critically understood by researchers. While there have been extensive studies on sustainable cities in Europe, the USA, and Asia (see for example, Al-Zu'bi & Radovic, 2018; Cohen, 2017; Caprotti & Yu, 2018, among others), the situation in contemporary Russian cities is totally unknown. However, Russia is one of the world's largest major emitters of greenhouse gases, as well as a leading global supplier of fossil fuels.

Despite some studies on the assessment of "greening" in Russia's cities, mostly written in the Russian language (see for example, Korotkov,

Trubyanov, Zagainova, & Nikonorov, 2015; Medvedeva, Kozenko, & Komarova, 2015, among others), there is a shortage of comprehensive studies performed in a qualitative paradigm. Such studies would, in addition to index assessment and generation of mathematical models, explain complex causal relationships and processes within a city, as well as identify the factors affecting the process of environmental decision-making from the perspectives of different urban stakeholders. This book addresses these gaps, offering a comprehensive empirically grounded interdisciplinary three-year study of the social-environmental situation and sustainability issues in Russian cities according to the international standards of a "sustainable" city.

The research, in the form of a case study of Moscow and Kazan, used a mixed methods approach. The rationale behind choosing the cities of Moscow and Kazan is based on their similarities and differences. They are the largest urban centers in Russia with a rapid innovative development and higher than average levels of education and income in comparison to other similar Russian cities. However, there are also differences in terms of geographic locations, the different structure of industrial and employment consolidations, and the different levels of environmental pollution and eco-conflicts. In both cities, a large number of innovative local initiatives led by municipalities and/or civil society aimed to improve the environment by reducing air and water pollution and providing efficient waste management and sustainable transport. Both cities have undergone significant recent urbanization and have higher than average levels of infrastructural advancements in comparison to other large Russian cities (P. Ermolaeva, Ermolaeva, Kuznetsova, Basheva, & Korunova, 2020). In both cities, civil society stands actively for the environment, including independent air pollution monitoring, protection of green and blue zones, protests against incineration plants, and initiatives around sustainable food consumption, cycling etc.

Desk research was used in the first stage to analyze the cities' profiles and their ecological, economic, technological, infrastructural, and social features linked to the "sustainability" agenda to assess the relevant sustainability ratings and statistics of both cities. The desk research also identified an initial group of stakeholders for the interviews while other stakeholders were identified through snowball sampling.

The analysis of mass media discourse allowed us to study how environmental discourse is portrayed and framed in the Russian mass media across two cases and identify the main claim-makers. To do so, we analyzed 10 national Russian online media which represent different perspectives: official (RIA Novosti, TASS, Rossiskaya Gazeta, informational agency RBC, Izvestya, Kommersant) and alternative (Meduza, Vedomosti, Mosckovsky Komsomolec, Novaya Gazeta).

All of the abovementioned newspapers are ranked among the most popular in Russia according to their audience numbers. The regional press is represented by six e-journals: M24.ru, RIAMO, mospravda.ru, Business-Online, Tatar-inform, Vechernya Kazan. The given newspapers were chosen because they have varying circulation figures and target audiences. The items from online media were studied from September 2017 to December 2018.

Purposive sampling, based on theoretical saturation, enabled the selection of 60 professionals for semi-structured interviews, including urban professionals, representatives of environmental non-governmental organizations (NGOs) and grassroots, academics, and regional proponents. The questions addressed the experts' in-depth assessments of the key features, challenges, and tendencies of sustainability transitions in selected Russian cases. The quantitative component of the study employed multi-stage stratified sampling to select representative samples of the Kazan and Moscow population aged 18 years and above (n = 1,500). The samples were representative of the cities' population with regard to gender, age, and geographic location. Interviews with professionals were conducted in 2018, and the survey was carried out in 2019.

The mixed methods approach allowed us the triangulation of "thick" contextual data and generalizable representative statistics to critically reflect on the behavioral, technological, and economic "readiness" of different groups of Russian citizens for transition to "sustainable" city standards, new environmental values, behaviors, and technologies.

Chapter 1. Russian Sustainable Cities: "Putting the Puzzle Together" opens with the authors' conceptual and methodological perspectives for studying sustainable cities in Russia. It provides an analysis of the historical, social, economic, and political contexts of their development. A critical analysis of the existing methodologies for measuring the sustainability of Russian cities is introduced as well as the key indicators that will be further conceptualized by the authors in the form of a puzzle.

Chapter 2. Puzzle 1: Air and Water Quality portrays the population and stakeholders' assessment along with hydrological monitoring on the quality of the air and water in Russian cities; it identifies the key problems and solutions.

Chapter 3. Puzzle 2: Sustainable Transport and Mobility provides critical reflections on the sustainability of transport and mobility systems in the post-soviet Russian landscape. The author portrays both positive and negative trends in the Russian transport system and its shift toward sustainability, including the cancellation of trolleybuses and tram routes, on the one hand, and the introduction of electric buses, new cycling trails and car-sharing programs, on the other.

Chapter 4. Puzzle 3: Energy Efficiency and Energy Consumption discusses the energy system of Russian cities, which was modeled on a centralized and affordable basis for every citizen and is controlled by state structures to ensure relatively low electricity consumption tariffs compared to Europe. The author shows citizens' attitudes and practices toward household energy consumption, key trends in the renewable energy market and acknowledges the major barriers to sustainability energy transitions such as energy justice and energy poverty issues, the infrastructural barriers, undeveloped "green" technologies, and the legal base.

Chapter 5. Puzzle 4: Waste Management provides a debate on the most controversial and urgent environmental issue for Russian cities– the problem of waste. The authors argue that for the last 20 years the waste management system in Russia has been in stagnation because there is a conflict among various groups, which try to lobby certain waste management technologies. The chapter also analyzes household waste consumption practices and the key challenges and "waste" conflicts in cities.

Chapter 6. Puzzle 5: Green and Blue Zones covers the issues of the "green" and "blue" infrastructure such as green spaces, rivers and lakes, stand condition and stability of plantings in the urban environment, accessibility of parks for citizens, creating parks and squares in residential areas, and providing care for them. Although these issues have become a priority for municipal authorities in the framework of urban development programs, citizens acknowledge certain problems which the chapter discusses.

Chapter 7. Puzzle 6: Environmental Governance and Politics demonstrates how grassroots groups and professional ecologists try to impact municipalities in situations of environmental "deinstitualization". It argues that the population has a high interest in environmental issues and uses various instruments to voice their concerns including social media, meetings, and petitions; however, the outcomes are uncertain.

The **Conclusion** section summarizes the main findings of the book and suggests strategies on how to promote sustainable cities in Russia based on the recommendations from key stakeholders' groups as well as the future prospects of the research under the new socio-economic and epidemiological risks.

1

RUSSIAN SUSTAINABLE CITIES: "PUTTING THE PUZZLE TOGETHER"

P. Ermolaeva, V. Korunova, O. Basheva, and Y. Ermolaeva

In the early 1990s, the Sustainable Cities Program by the UN is being established. It implies the creation of "sustainable cities" through the means of powerful local governments and the active participation of all parties concerned. In 1999, the UN published guidelines on the creation of institutes for eco-friendly city management (UN-Habitat-Nairobi, KE, United Nations Human Settlements Program, & UNEP-Nairobi, KE., 1999). The incremental reappraisal of capitalist values and economic recession also provided the impetus for the search for alternative forms of socio-economic development of the society. The concept of a sustainable city appeared, one of the most common sustainable urban development concepts nowadays (Pickett et al., 2013). A sustainable city adheres to the strategy of a long-term and balanced social, economic, and material-and-technical development, where natural resources are used efficiently and acceptable levels of the human impact on the environment are established (Hamman, Anquetin, & Monicolle, 2017; Karlenzig, 2007). The main concepts of sustainable urban development are "Garden City," "Ecocity," "Compact City," "Low Carbon City," "Green City," "Sustainable City," and "Smart Sustainable City"(Caprotti, 2014).

Because of the drastic changes in the social order of Russia and critical states (wars, changes in the forms of social production), no single development pathway of a sustainable city concept could form in the Russian science and practices. Many of the Russian scientists' ideas were borrowed from their Western colleagues, but it is also possible to track the development of original concepts distinctive to the Russian context. Researchers have noted (Yanitsky

& Usacheva, 2017) that almost none of the sustainability concepts were implemented fully by Russian city planners for various reasons (resource issues, organizational troubles, etc.).

In Russia, sustainable city concepts stem from Vernadsky's concept of a noosphere (Vernadsky, 1991). Scholars and practitioners of environmental protection looked for more efficient approaches to the optimization of natural resource use, from modeling the management of complex regional and global processes of transition to the noosphere to developing resource-efficient and low-waste technologies. They were looking for eco-friendly approaches to urban development in the areas of management, education, technologies, and construction. Still, as territories and economies grew, such approaches were becoming increasingly difficult to implement. This is why the only significant results of a comprehensive ecologization were achieved at the level of rare individual enterprises and their subordinate settlements in the USSR (Basheva, 2017).

In Russia, before the revolution of 1917, Howard's garden city concept was applied when designing suburban residential and dacha settlements commonly deprived of an industrial zone. This concept found its realization in such towns as Chaykovsky in Perm Krai, Slavutych in Kyiv Oblast (built for the evacuated personnel of the Chernobyl Nuclear Power Plant), resort towns, scientific centers (Zelenograd, Pushchino), and closed towns with little production other than constructions and municipal services. In Russia, a garden city concept was perceived as an opportunity to create green and well-adjusted to the environment suburban residential settlements with low-rise dwellings. Several projects of such garden settlements were developed, even though the most outstanding of them remained unfulfilled. In the Soviet era, Howard's ideas were first supported, but by the end of the 1920s, they underwent ideological criticism and prohibition because the concept of a garden city turned out to be incompatible with the institutional and management doctrine of the Soviet authorities (Meerovich, 2009).

Among the Russian concepts of ecologization, combining both theoretical and practical aspects, Ecopolis Program of Pushchino is the best known (1980–1985, Ekologiya malogo goroda, 1981; Safroshkin, 1991). A special committee was formed to develop a program of comprehensive urban ecologization called Ecopolis. An "ecopolis" is a new-generation city practising the conjugated development of the nature and the society The intended result was the creation of an ecologically and psychologically optimal environment consistent with the needs of a human as a biological and social being and permitting the existence of natural ecosystems in the city and nature (Safroshkin, 1991). For a city, the main principles are represented by environmental upbringing and education and eco-oriented practices of the population and authorities.

In the early 1980s, the concept of a Biotic City developed by Tetior was proposed (Tetior, 2016, 2017). Settlements are supposed to feature favorable conditions for the existence of all living beings, including flora, fauna, and humans. The all-inclusive development of flora and fauna in a city is considered essential for the comprehensive development of a human as a representative of the living world and nature. Tetior outlined the principles of biopositivity, or ecologization of human activity, such as negentropy, homeostatic equilibrium with the environment, equivalent substitution, biosphere compatibility, deep bio-analogy, ecological support, environmental restoration, beauty, harmony, and proportion with nature (Basheva, 2017).

Since the mid-1990s, as part of the "Environmental Cities of the Future" project, efforts have been made to ecologize historical Russian cities, such as Tobolsk, Kirishi, Tikhvin, etc. The ecologization concept inherent in the project overall matches the global tendencies implying the transition toward the sustainable urban development (Grigoriev & Ogorodnikov, 2001). The project unites several programs aimed at the ecologization of the said cities and tackling a wide range of city-planning and social matters, such as immediate city-planning issues, the issues of land-utilization, urban environmental monitoring, urban landscape renovation, waste removal, energy-saving, utilization of alternative energy sources, purity of air and water, transportation, public participation in the ecologization of the city, managing legal aspects, and developing eco-friendly businesses.

In 1996, Russia officially confirmed its participation in implementing the global sustainable development concept. In Russia, the principles of sustainable urban development are found in numerous strategic documents, federal and regional laws, the strategic development plan of the country and its territories. They serve as the key component of Goal 11, "Make cities and human settlements inclusive, safe, resilient and sustainable," of the United Nations Agenda 2030 for Sustainable Development. However, there is no systematic or consistent implementation of the principles of the sustainable development of Russian territories with laws and regulations. At the governmental level, sustainability is perceived to satisfy the need of the government and the society in the economic well-being and development and the realization of smart, sustainable city goals in the digitalization of the urban environment.

The main provisions of this concept were reflected in the most comprehensive way in the National Environmental Action Plan of the Russian Federation for 1999–2001 that did not receive sufficient legal power. The Federal Environmental Protection Law and the Ecological Doctrine of the

Russian Federation enacted in 2002 include the principles of transitioning to sustainability, and goals, objectives, and areas of focus based on the environmental policy principles. Besides, the Environmental Doctrine also attributes particular importance to the sustainable development of regions, which served for the development and enactment of the Federal Target Program "Sustainable Rural Development in 2014–2017 and for the period until 2020" in 2013. However, the mechanisms intended for the solution of the issues listed in these documents are not compliant with the sustainable development requirements.

The complexity of finding a compromise between the ecologization of life and ensuring the economic development of the country serves as the main reason for the absence of an approved strategic document stipulating the transition to sustainable development, work on which began after a corresponding Presidential order in 1994 (Shelekhov, 2002). Instead, the Environmental Security Strategy of the Russian Federation until 2025 was accepted in 2025. It includes such public policy objectives as environmental preservation and restoration and ensuring the high quality of the environment for the well-being of people and sustainable economic development (Kremlin.ru, 2017). Later, the quality of the urban environment was also referred to the possibility of performing open remote management, or smart management, reflected in the smart city concept enacted in 2018 (The Center for Strategic Research "North-West", 2018).

The goal of this project is the development of a smart, sustainable city where the system of informational and communicational technologies ensures high living standards through the establishment of smart energy and mobility systems and smart solutions in the areas of medicine, education, construction, safety, environmental protection, etc. In compliance with these requirements, the project enacted in Russia is aimed at increasing the effectiveness of the urban environment comprehensively, including the creation of a competitive, manageable, technologically advanced, safe, and comfortable infrastructure (Ministry of Construction, Housing and Utilities of the Russian Federation, n.d.).

But the stipulated objectives feature fewer comprehensive solutions. Thus, according to the analytical report on implementing smart technologies in Russian cities, the majority of projects realized nowadays are characterized by strict localization (The Center for Strategic Research "North-West", 2018). It is mostly reflected in placing greater focus on the smart resolution of the issues of basic computerization, public security, and transportation and its energy efficiency, as over 80% of all projects implemented in Russia are aimed at tackling these matters. In comparison, the share of projects aimed at improving the environmental situation and optimizing the waste management system constitutes as little as 4%. Geographically speaking, only one-fifth of all Russian cities make certain steps toward smart sustainability from the viewpoint of its environmental component.

Nowadays, the possibilities of introducing smart technologies are provisionally discussed in most Russian territorial subjects, and in some, respective legislative projects have been enacted, for example, in the towns of Moscow (TAdviser, 2020), Saint Petersburg (Tishchenko, 2018), Sevastopol (Pravitelstvo Sevastopolya, n.d.), and Yuzhno-Sakhalinsk (Ob utverzhdenii koncepcii, 2019), and in Ulyanovsk (Koncepciya vnedreniya, 2017) and Sverdlovsk Oblasts ('Umnyj region' — SMART REGION, 2018).

Aside from them, greenfield initiatives also include the creation of small innovative towns and districts, such as Skolkovo science city in Moscow, Yuzhny satellite town in Saint Petersburg, SMART City, and Innopolis satellite towns in Kazan, and Akademicheskiy microdistrict in Yekaterinburg. However, in expert opinion, no projects can be deemed successful. SMART City, a green city development project from Tatarstan, serves as the most prominent example. It was one of the first attempts to perform comprehensive smart territory planning in Russia in 2012. According to the plan, SMART City is a smart, sustainable city combining the features of an international social and business and academic centers, and a special economic and park zone, which ensures the high quality of life for the residents, and, contributes to the sustainable economic development of the region (Durnitsyna, 2013). But SMART City project is closed because of investment complications, just like another greenfield project, Innopolis (Proekt 'Smart siti Kazan', 2015).

From a conceptual perspective, the sustainable city concept is equated with the sustainable development concept in the context of Russia. Despite the widespread acceptance of such a term as "sustainable city" in the scientific literature of the world, this notion remains to be insufficiently formalized in the Russian practice and is used in different interpretations (P. Ermolaeva, Yanitsky, Basheva, Ermolaeva, & Kuznetsova, 2019). This is why, drawing on the global and Russian experience, in this book, we define "sustainable city" as a city combining high efficiency and innovativeness; a city where the population is provided with the best living conditions (given exiting restrictions and opportunities); a city that persists through constant change. The term "sustainable city" implies both an environmentally friendly city, a city congenial for the population, and its other inhabitants, and a complex of social conditions and factors that should be considered when designing cities depending on their geographic location, population, and functions (P. Ermolaeva et al., 2019).

The main characteristic that should be addressed when studying and designing the model of sustainable cities in Russia is their structural and functional organization becoming increasingly dependent on the domestic and international geopolitical processes (Yanitsky, 2018a). These processes are represented by the competition for resources, the competition for the stability of the existing political system in the country, and the simultaneous competition for the geopolitical dominance in the world; accelerating technological advancement; global market laws; the growing gap between the rich and the poor; the worsening of the environmental conditions; and new global challenges (the climate change, COVID-19 pandemic, etc.). Nowadays, Russian mega-cities are transitioning from the industrial to the post-industrial model, where the key role is played by informational and communicational processes. The rapid technological advancement of mega-cities comes with the incremental growth of two types of risks. There are external risks, for example, global warming, the coronavirus pandemic, or the threat of armed conflict, and internal risks stemming from the dynamics of the mega-cities themselves.

In this book, the main methodological frameworks for considering the transition of Russian cities to sustainable city standards employed by us are the approach of socio-biotechnical (SBT) systems (Efremenko, Yanitsky, & Ermolaeva, 2019; Yanitsky, 2018b), environmental inequality theories in waste studies (Gonzalez, 2013), socio-psychological theories of the environmental behavior (P. Ermolaeva & Ermolaeva, 2019; Schwartz, 1977; Stern, 2005), the zero-waste concept, and the principles of a circular economy (Murray, 2002).

We consider a city to be a SBT system, that is, an open system of non-linear connections and interactions, in which technical, environmental, and social aspects act as integral characteristics of a whole (Efremenko et al., 2019; Yanitsky, 2018b). English-speaking scientific literature commonly employs the term "interaction" (Diani, 2003). It is sufficient to describe and analyze the social interactions in the material and virtual form. However, a city is a complex and indivisible network of natural, social, and technological processes. This is the main qualitative difference of cities from natural processes, including the cycle of matter in nature. However, they have something in common, the reciprocal impact of different matters (processes, systems). All these interactions make qualitative changes to one another. This is why the city, having appeared as the opposite of the natural system, unites with it on the one hand and with the technological processes and their infrastructure on the other. This is why we consider the changes of urban systems to be, first, complex, dynamic, systematic (the changes occur in several systems simultaneously), and non-linear processes; second, the trajectories of changes originate from the interactions between multiple systems, which cannot be reviewed within the scope of mono-disciplinary approaches. All types of SBT systems, regardless of their scale, are considered conflicting, contradictory, and internally riskogenic in their nature. These characteristics are conditioned by the competition for dominance and resources, the conflict of short-term political success and long-term trends, and the diversity of social, biospheric, and technological components. These characteristics are also associated with the varying degree of information on their riskogenics and the manageability of their components.

The ideological vector in the analysis of waste generation and management is represented by the zero-waste concept (Murray, 2002) that is based on two major principles of zero waste and zero loss, and several other principles. They are the establishment of a circular or zero-waste economy that implies the recovery of recycled materials for reuse (Von Weizsäcker, Hargrouz, & Smith, 2013); the establishment of a circular or zero-waste economy where the indicators showing the reduction of negative impact on the environment are included into the financial cost (Bobylev & Solovyeva, 2017; Ren21, 2011); the establishment of technological cycles and environmental parks intended to transition the production and consumption lifecycles from linear to circular; and the establishment of new social capital forms supporting the zero-waste economy (for example, "green" workplaces, the environmental equality, etc.). Within the scope of this work, we interviewed experts, surveyed the population, and analyzed the media and official public reports because it was important for us to understand how experts interpret the zero-waste concept in Russia given the characteristic combination of different management schemes and urban needs of the country (European Environment Agency, 2013; Yanitsky & Usacheva, 2017).

When analyzing the situation in Russia, the balance of the generated waste is revised with due regard to resource efficiency that implies a social component represented by active agents and social structures, a list of environmental challenges, and propositions on improving the situation voiced by proactive structures. The more effective a community is in using various types of raw materials and energy when transforming them and distributing the final product, the higher its cultural, technological, and economical capacity is (Y. Ermolaeva, 2015). At the forefront of our research are the interactions between the ecotechnological systems and the culture and the interactions between material and non-material flows and their transformations (Y. Ermolaeva, 2015; United Nations, 2015a).

We used the environmental justice concept to analyze modern environmental conflicts in Russia triggered by the appearance of landfills and waste incineration plants, and the export of waste from Moscow to the neighboring territories (Gonzalez, 2013; Pellow, 2002). It allows us to focus on determining the minorities sensitive to the sources of environmental pollution (proximity to dumping sites, waste incineration plants, landfills, sites with the underground disposal of toxic substances, etc.). It suggests equal access to a non-polluted environment, ensuring occupational safety and high-living standards for the city dwellers regardless of the socio-demographic indicators. It allowed us to clearly identify the social groups suffering from the ecological damage and to review the tools and initiatives that help them create a more comfortable environment for themselves. According to Ulrich Beck (1992),

> *...the lower class of the social strata is more likely to be exposed to harmful substances given the lack of financial possibilities to move from the polluted areas, purchase eco-friendly products, or go on vacation regularly. As a rule, people of this class are unable to refuse unsafe work due to the fear of losing their job; finally, due to being undereducated and poorly informed, they know very little of the environmental hazards and the means of reducing them.*

In our work, we employed the heuristic possibilities of pro-environmental behavior theories to gain an insight into the environmental mindset, motives, and practices of households. We addressed the contextual theory suggested by Paul Stern (2000) to determine the reasons for population's (non)involvement in eco-friendly practices, separate waste collection practices in particular. According to this theory, a person's determination to be involved in environmentally responsible behavior results from numerous diverse factors, such as economic, socio-altruistic, socio-egocentric, situational, etc. Aside from the internal factors associated with the environmental consciousness, there are external factors involving many external powers that do not depend on individual preferences, mindsets, and convictions, such as the economic situation, the infrastructural and socio-cultural support of reproducing eco-friendly values and practices, a network of environmental organizations, environmental legislation, environmental monitoring, etc.

Over the past decade, several comprehensive types of research on urban sustainability were conducted in Russia. Some adapted foreign models, while others employed a unique methodological apparatus of Russian researchers. For example, they are the works by Korotkov and Trubyanov (2014), Bobylev, Kudryavtseva, and Solovyova (2014), etc.

Korotkov and Trubyanov (2014) emphasized the necessity of discovering models that would ensure economic growth while lowering the damage to the environment and natural resources. Based on a case study of large administrative centers of the Russian regions, a methodology of a quantitative assessment of the ecological effectiveness of cities was developed; then it was applied to draw a rating of Russian cities. The methodology is designed for large cities exclusively and requires complete official statistical data, which is often unavailable for several cities.

Medvedeva, Kozenko, and Komarova (2015) suggested a conceptual and methodological foundation for the strategy of developing sustainable cities based on medium-sized industrialized Russian cities. Researchers distinguished the factors influencing the state and the vector of development of a middle-sized city (organizational and administrative, technical and technological, infrastructural, ecological, tourist and recreational, informational and communicational, and social). They proposed a methodology of calculating an integral index assessing the developmental potential of a middle-sized city regarding the promotion of "green" technologies. This index includes the evaluation of industrial, manufacturing, infrastructural, financial, and human potential.

Bobylev et al. (2014) adjusted city sustainability indicators to the Russian context based on the human development index of the UN Development Program and the adjusted net savings (ANS) index by the World Bank. To assess the sustainability of developing a city, while considering the economic, social, and ecological factors, the authors propose to distinguish three respective sub-indexes: gross fixed capital formation, human capital development expenses, and the damages caused by the environmental pollution in cities. Researchers proposed the key indicators reflecting major economic, social, and environmental priorities, which they divided into nine groups: economic indicators, energetic effectiveness, transport, social and institutional indicators, air and climate, water resources, waste, specially protected natural reservations, and noise impact. According to the authors, this indicator system reflects the most relevant problems of the sustainable development of Russian cities and the quality of life of their citizens. It is also suitable for the possibilities of Russian statistics.

A group of researchers developed an Integral Index of City Sustainability. It is based on the concept and calculation technique of the ANS index by the World Bank. They also used as a methodological and statistical base the results of a project by the World Wide Fund for Nature Russia and RIA Novosti that the researchers participated in to develop and calculate the environmental-economic index of Russian regions. To assess the sustainability of a developing city, while considering the economic, social, and ecological factors, the authors propose to distinguish three respective sub-indexes: gross fixed capital formation, human capital development expenses (for example, education, healthcare, physical culture, and sports), and the damages caused by the environmental pollution in cities (for example, the damage of air pollution and CO_2 emissions affecting the climate).

These sub-indexes are the aggregates of several indicators and their calculation can be determined by the accessibility of statistical data and aggregation purposes.

City sustainability index or the index of ANS for cities can be calculated according to the following formula, where all components are presented as a percentage of the gross regional product or its statistical analog for cities.

$$ANS = GS + HCB - ED,$$

where GS is gross savings, HCB stands for the human capital budget, and ED represents the economic damage from environmental pollution.

The results show the generalized calculations of the city sustainability index for Moscow and Saint Petersburg. The choice of these cities is conditioned by the relative simplicity of calculations given the accessibility of statistics at the federal level, especially the regular gross regional product calculations performed by Rosstat. To calculate the economic damage from environmental pollution, the damage standards used by the World Bank and the European Community and adjusted for Russia were employed. The findings show that Saint Petersburg features a more sustainable development than Moscow, primarily through the economic component of higher value represented by the index of gross savings. The human capital budget as a percentage of GRP is also higher in Saint Petersburg. The relative economic damage from environmental pollution is lower in Moscow.

Another methodology developed supported by the Russian Geographical Society is based on the consideration of statistically significant characteristics of anthropogenic impact, and the power and technological features of its sources. This methodology considers international recommendations and the experience of similar ratings of other countries, and therefore focuses on four priority areas of anthropogenic impact (on the atmosphere, water and land resources, heat and radiation exposure) and uses a few quantitative sub-indices for each (Kasimov, 2014).

Aside from the proprietary methodologies mostly performed by economists, several corporate methodologies assess the sustainability of Russian cities that employ the data provided by Rosstat and other government structures. For example, there are assessments based on the air pollution level (Rejting rossijskih gorodov, 2013) and the attraction of the urban environment (V Rossii sostavlen, 2013), the integral rating of the largest Russian cities (Kolesova, 2014), the sustainability rating of Russian cities by SGM agency (SGM, 2015), the rating of the environmental management of Russian cities annually drawn by the subordinate authorities of Minprirodi RF with the methodological support of EY, a British accounting and consulting firm (Rejting ekologicheskogo upravleniya, 2015), and the environmental development rating of Russian cities (Rejting ekologicheskogo razvitiya, 2017).

The «Urbanika» Institute has developed an integrated rating of comfort and affordability of life in Russian cities. The data of the Federal State Statistics Service, the Ministry of Internal Affairs, real estate market consultants, and climatic indicators of the area are used to assess the quality of the urban environment (housing, the availability of modern trade formats, urban roads congestion, crime, urban amenities, lighting, favorable climatic conditions, transport accessibility, and atmospheric pollution index), and the cost of maintaining it (based on the average wage in the city, the possibility of acquiring your housing, renting a one-room apartment, and current expenses, expenses for housing and communal services, and the purchasing power of citizens), each giving 50 rating points (with a maximum of 100) (Fedorova, 2019). A different methodology lies, for example, based on the ranking of the ecological well-being of Russian cities, calculated by "Domofond.ru" analysts based on a population survey. So, citizens are invited to determine the degree of their agreement with the statement "My city has enough greenery and clean fresh air" on a 10-point scale, and in free form, to comment on the observed situation, which allows us to get a quantitative and qualitative assessment of the state of the environment in cities from their inhabitants (Domofond.ru, 2018).

The methodology assessing the sustainable development of Russian cities designed by the SGM agency is one of the most popular (SGM, 2015). The rating was first drawn in 2012 under the principles of the sustainable development of a territory determined by international organizations, such as McKinsey, Ernst & Young, PWC, etc., and the scientific community. The rating is designed for cities with populations of over 100,000 people. The positions of cities in the rating are determined based on 32 indicators assessing three major sectors of sustainable development, such as the economic, environmental, and social sector (including demographics). The economic block of indicators evaluates the state of the manufacturing sector, the volume of investments, the job market, the income level of the population, the economic performance of enterprises, and the balance of municipal budgets. The advancement of the city infrastructure is assessed helped by indicators characterizing the city's housing stock, the rate of new housing supply, the performance of the heat supply scheme, and the level of development of public transportation, which is especially significant for larger cities. The assessment of the environmental condition of a city considers the air pollution levels and the environmental performance of enterprises. To assess the demographic situation, population growth rates and the demographic burden are used. The block of indicators evaluating the development of the social infrastructure considers the accessibility of educational and healthcare services and the safety level of cities. All primary data used to draw the rating of cities are available in public access.

In Autumn of 2017, experts from the All-Russia People's Front in association with the Ministry of Natural Resources of Russia prepared yet another "Environmental rating of Russian cities" based on the data provided by the authorities of large municipal entities on the territory of all regions of the country (Ministry of Natural Resources and Environment of the Russian Federation, 2017a). The particular characteristic of this rating is that aside from the quantitative data, expert and public opinions were considered to get a full picture. The environmental rating of Russian cities is designed by Green Patrol, a non-profit environmental organization (National Environmental Rating). Its goal is to exercise public monitoring and comparative assessment of Russian regions in environmental safety and protection. The rating is calculated online. The data bank of the informational and analytical system registers significant events. There is a History of Events available for every region that reflects such significant events. The advantage of this rating lies in it not only being just based on statistical data but also considers the evaluation proposed by the proactive locals and registers the events online, which makes it unique for multilevel analysis. The compilation system of this rating is typically characterized by its results being relative and depend on the indicators of all the subjects participating in the rating over a covered period. The position of a particular region in the rating may vary throughout different periods, while its indicators are the same, because of the changes in the indicators of other regions.

The analysis showed that all calculating methodologies, except for the methodology by Green Patrol, are based on quantitative (statistical) data, which is their advantage, on the one hand, as it makes their results objective, but is also a shortcoming as it is impossible to track the annual dynamics of the indicators because of the delayed publishing of statistics or their absence. In addition, the difficulty of choosing the most suitable dynamics resides in significant changes in developing big, medium, and small cities in Russia; most rating methodologies are designed only for one type of city. While pointing out the significant amount of existing foreign and Russian studies on the assessment of urban sustainability, there are no interdisciplinary works assessing the degree of greening of Russian cities based on the analysis of objective indicators, subjective opinions of different groups of the urban stakeholders, and expert opinions. Also, the above-mentioned methodologies are limited as it is impossible to track the dynamics of the urban sustainability.

Considering these limitations, the authors' methodology of assessing the sustainability of Russian cities is characterized by the quantitative statistical approach being supplemented by the sociological approach based on the diagnostics of values, practices, and motives of different groups of urban population and the expert opinions. In this book, we focused on assessing the indicators of the socio-environmental sustainability of Russian cities. The following were deemed to be the main indicators: the air and water quality, sustainable transportation and mobility, energy efficiency and consumption, waste management, green and blue zones, and environmental governance and politics. In the upcoming chapters, we will reflect on each indicator in greater detail.

2

PUZZLE 1: AIR AND WATER QUALITY

I. Kuznetsova and V. Korunova

The results of air quality monitoring in Russia at the beginning of 2020 demonstrated a 57% growth of pollution in comparison with 2019. The number of cases of water pollution, instead, dropped by 30% (Finexpertiza, 2020). Despite the high level of water accessibility in Russia with 96% of the urban population in Russia having piped water and 96% of the overall population having access to water free from contamination, the indicator of "safely managed water supplies" is problematic as only 76% of the population has such access (Progress on household, 2019, p. 101). The pollution of rivers is a point of high concern as well, as in the majority of river ecosystems or segments of river systems in European Russia, water is classified as polluted, very polluted, or dirty (Nikanorov et al., 2016, p. 802). The level of air pollution is very high, but the data from official monitoring are not transparent, nor the methodology of the monitoring accurate, despite the fact that public health studies demonstrate the high risks of respiratory, cardiovascular, and oncological diseases caused by air pollution in Moscow and Kazan.

This chapter provides empirical data about the perceptions of air and water quality and pollution held by the population and professionals of Moscow and Kazan. It shows how air pollution became more politicized since the construction of an incineration plant near Kazan and air pollution caused by landfills in Moscow oblast, while water quality stays a less politicized aspect of the environment.

AIR QUALITY: CONTESTED MONITORING, FACTORS OF POLLUTION AND POLICIES

The main sources of air pollution in Russia are from enterprises in the metallurgical, mining, oil, and pulp and paper industries, as well as in the field of housing and communal services. Therefore, the regions with a high concentration of heavy industries are the most affected and include Buryatia, Transbaikalia, and Krasnoyarsk territory (Finexpertiza, 2020). Officially, Moscow and Kazan are not among the most air polluted regions in Russia. Also, according to a comparison of Moscow with some other cities in the world, in most of the indicators, it is not at the top in terms of air pollution (Moscow Mayor Official web-site, 2019b). The official monitoring data provided by the Moscow City Government shows that

> *...over the past 8 years, the average annual concentration of carbon monoxide and nitric oxide decreased by 2.1 times in the city. A gradual decline in the concentration of nitrogen dioxide and PM10 and PM2.5 suspended substances was documented.*
>
> *(Moscow Mayor Official web-site, 2019b, p. 228).*

While the official data showed a low level of air pollution according to the standard regulations in Kazan in 2016 (Ministry of Ecology and Natural Resources of the Republic of Tatarstan, 2017), in 2018, the level of air pollution was considered to be elevated there (V dvukh gorodakh RT, 2019).

Talking about the normalization of air quality in the cities studied during our research would be premature not only due to the negative tendencies observed in Kazan but also due to the fact that the maximum permissible concentrations of formaldehyde and phenol were increased in 2014–2015 (by three and two times, respectively). Moreover, the limit for the daily permissible average MPC for methanethiol (which is also generated at landfills) was lowered by 660 times in 1999–2017 and by 60 times over the past 10 years. Greenpeace published an open letter to Russian official institutions demanding they should reconsider the norms (Greenpeace.ru, 2019), but the request for action has not been taken into consideration.

At the same time, alternative monitoring performed by Greenpeace with the help of volunteers in eight Russian cities, including Moscow and Kazan, showed a high level of air pollution in isolated districts, including highways (see for example, Yukhnovskaya, 2018). Around 4,150 complaints have been recorded on the Greenpeace interactive map SOS! Vozdukh (SOS!Air), with 1,200 being uploaded by the population of Moscow oblast, and 800 by

Muscovites (Greenpeace.ru, 2020). Also, the data from public health studies in Russia demonstrate that oxygen deficiency caused by air pollution impacts on respiratory and cardiovascular diseases, and carcinogens in the air impact on the increase of oncological diseases (see Boytsov et al., 2016; Revich, Avaliani, & Simons, 2016; Revich & Shaposhnikov, 2010). For example, in Kazan, there is a high level of health risk caused by the air pollution (Tafeyeva, Ivanov, Titova, & Akhmetzyanova, 2015, p. 37).

Air pollution in Russian cities is affected by a number of factors. First, it is the consequence of Soviet industrialization and the location of environmentally harmful production processes in cities or in close proximity to them. Second, air pollution factors are insufficiently considered in spatial planning. In 2019, Federal Law 195 introduced amendments to the Town Planning Code of Russia and, in isolated cases, required planning approval by the executive government body of the constituent entity of the Russian Federation in charge of the protection of atmospheric air. However, the amendments are mostly associated with the placement of facilities emitting pollutants in the air and do not provide any regulation for the streets that are becoming overwhelmed with private and public vehicles, which leads to air pollution. Third, the lack of an eco-friendly system of waste management results in the accumulation of waste at landfills near inhabited areas and the construction of waste incineration plants. Fourth, the system of eco-friendly public transportation is underdeveloped. Fifth, there is social inequality manifested by the fact that eco-friendly transportation is unaffordable for most citizens and by the lack of workplaces in small towns which leads to the internal migration of masses to Moscow and regional capitals and an increase in the traffic load.

In 2018, Russia adopted a federal program "Clean Air" as part of the national project "Ecology" which aims to control the quality of air across the country and includes a reduction of at least 20% in the total amount of pollutant emissions in the air in the most polluted cities. However, the effectiveness of this program is limited because the current system of monitoring does not allow the sources of pollution to be found in real-time (Paramonova, 2020); also it does not include a proper system of law enforcement. Moreover, regions have not received funding for the implementation of the "Clean Air" project in 2018–2019 (Ivantsova, 2019).

Vehicle emissions are a main cause of air pollution in Moscow (Elansky, Shilkin, Ponomarev, Semutnikova, & Zakharova, 2020; Klyuev, 2019), together with the operation of central heating systems, and in spring, the suspensions of anti-icing chemical reagents and soil particles lifted into the air (Elansky et al., 2020). Also, as Klyuev argues, there is a lack of environmental concern in territorial development. Transport is responsible for the increased concentration of nitrogen dioxide, carbon monoxide, and sulfur dioxide. Moreover, it was noted that the functioning of industrial enterprises negatively affects the air quality since it increases the concentration of hydrogen sulfide and ammonia. Waste incineration plants are also responsible for increased air toxicity. Experts noted the possible negative consequences of placing such enterprises in the Moscow region. Overall, the air quality was assessed by experts as satisfactory in both cities by official sources. In Kazan, real-time data on air quality are published daily, while in Moscow, the publication of similar information has been discontinued by Mosekomonitoring since 2017 due to site modernization. The latter has been objected to by Greenpeace and other environmental organizations.

ATTITUDES TOWARD AIR POLLUTION AMONG POPULATION AND PROTESTS AGAINST WASTE INCINERATION PLANTS

In recent years, air pollution has become highly politicized and caused mass protests and ecological activism in both regions. Opposition was focused against hydrogen sulfide release in a waste plant – an open-air landfill site – at Yadrovo near Volokolamsk (Moscow oblast) in 2018. In other areas near Moscow, thousands of people have defied police bans to march against planned landfill openings, blaming the mounting piles of garbage for health problems and foul-smelling air (see the Chapter 5 "Waste management" in this book). In Tatarstan, since 2017, there have been protests against the construction of the waste incineration plant in a village called Osinovo, near Kazan. The residents were primarily showing concern about air pollution. Despite the Supreme Court of the Republic of Tatarstan instructing the Cabinet to conduct public hearings devoted to the subject, they were conducted without the opportunity for all registered people to be present, and the activists did not have a chance to put forward their opinions (Gimalova, 2018). The protests continued, but the project was approved in 2020 following a project review by an international company. Experts from the German company stated that the plant "cannot cause significant damage or cause harmful effects on the environment" (Proyekt musoroszhigatel'nogo, 2020). Subsequently, the construction of the waste plant is on its way despite strong local opposition against it from the several thousand people who live in the village.

Despite the concerns regarding air pollution and protests by people living near landfills and near proposed sites for waste incineration plants, on average, the majority of the surveyed urban population shows little concern about air quality. Only about one fifth of the respondents showed serious concern for the air quality in their residential area (18.7%), 43.1% indicated that it "worries them a little", and 28.7% said that they are untroubled by it. Those who showed concern for the air quality noted that, in order to minimize the effect of poor air quality on themselves, they spent their time in rural areas and in parks (51.3%), kept their windows closed (16.3%), and used air ionizers (14.6%). A total of 15.6% indicated that they tried to find a residential district with higher air quality to live in. Slightly over one fifth of the respondents stated that they felt there was nothing they could do (21.9%) (Fig.2.1). At the same time, the surveyed population in Moscow provided lower evaluation of air quality comparing with the population of Kazan (2.96 vs 3.19 in a 5 grades scale). One third of Muscovites and 29.9% of the population of Kazan think that the air quality has decreased in the recent five years. Only 13% of those surveyed in Moscow and 14% of respondents in Kazan believe that the air quality has improved.

Mitigation practices to decrease the negative impact of air pollution are not accessible for people with fewer resources, those who do not have a dacha (a summer house) or money to spend time in the suburbs on a weekend. Lack of resources limits opportunities to move apartments to escape the effects of pollution as well. Also, as air quality monitoring has shown, mass travel of Muscovites from the city to their country houses on weekends impacts on air pollution (Elansky et al., 2020).

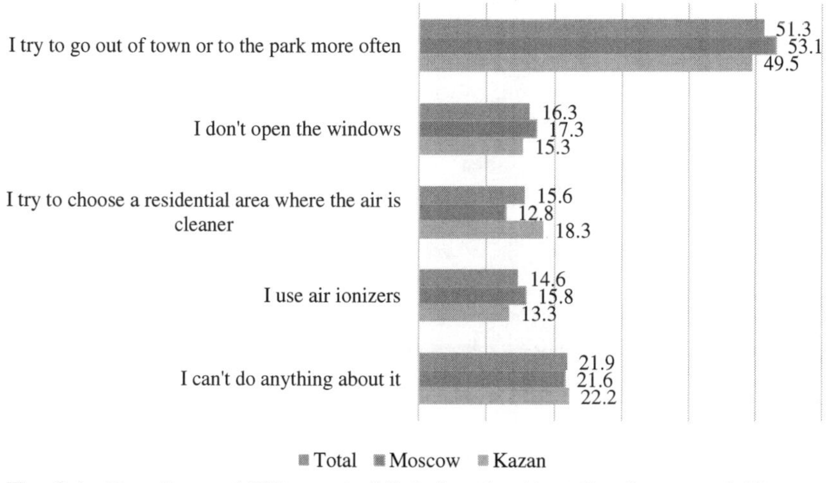

Fig. 2.1. Practices of Citizens to Minimize the Negative Impact of Air Pollution (%).

The problem of air pollution caused by waste incineration plants and the following protests have been extensively represented by the mass media both at regional and federal levels (see P. Ermolaeva, Ermolaeva, Kuznetsova, Basheva, & Korunova, 2020). Nevertheless, complex air pollution factors and the means of overcoming the growing levels of air pollution are not regularly covered in the media. Mass media did not represent the factors of persistent atmospheric pollution in Russian cities as a long-term problem was not viewed as "urgent" and of interest to the general public. There is a lack of regular discussions in the mass media about various factors of air pollution and its mitigation.

CURRENT CONDITION AND TRENDS IN THE DEVELOPMENT OF THE RUSSIAN WATER SUPPLY SYSTEM

According to data in the state report "On the condition of the sanitary and epidemiological well-being of the Russian population in 2017", 94.5% of the urban population was provided with safe water from central water supply systems in 2017. The share of public drinking water supply sources non-compliant with the sanitary-epidemiological requirements fell to 15.2% by 2017, while the corresponding number of water supply pipes decreased by 7.9%. The composition of tap water also improved overall in Russia, especially according to microbiologic and parasitological indicators (Gosudarstvennyy doklad, 2018).

Despite the high load, the quality of water supply in Moscow is high enough according to the authorities. For example, in 2015, Moscow was included in the top 10 of cities with the best water quality according to the Ministry of Environment and Natural Resources of Russia (Rejting ekologicheskogo upravleniya, 2015). The water quality in Moscow is also assessed positively by the experts included in the survey, who awarded it the score of 3.4 out of 5. In their opinion, the quality of tap water in Moscow is higher than that in the majority of other Russian cities, "I consider the quality of water to be high enough, I think it is safe to drink it, and I am satisfied with the quality of water purification" (a professional environmentalist, Moscow); "Water is good in Moscow… It is indeed much better than in many other Russian cities" (a business representative, Moscow).

The quality of the water supply in Kazan is rather low, despite the fact that the load is also lower than in Moscow. Experts gave its quality the score of 2.8. In the experts' opinion, the tap water in Kazan is safe, but its taste leaves much to be desired: "The water quality is hardly ideal. Nevertheless, I am not concerned about this water being unsafe" (a representative of the scientific community, Kazan); "I cannot say that I have good tap water at home. However, what matters is that it's safe" (a professional environmentalist, Kazan).

Locals share the same opinion on this. Muscovites consider the quality of their tap water to be average (3.35 out of 5), as well as its taste (3.29). The color and smell of the tap water were assessed higher by the population (3.85 and 3.56, respectively). However, they are rather cautious when using it for cooking and drinking. The majority of the respondents filter tap water (38.4%) or boil it (31.9%), and a smaller share of the population prefers to buy bottled water (22.9%). A total of 6.3% of the surveyed Muscovites drink and cook with tap water.

The citizens of Kazan also consider the quality of their tap water to be average (3.1 out of 5), as well as its smell (3.2) and color (3.45). The people in the survey assessed the taste of tap water in Kazan to be below average (2.9 out of 5), which is why only 4.8% of the population drink and cook with tap water. Two thirds of the respondents first filter (34.8%) or boil (31.7%) tap water before using it. Bottled water is more used by the citizens of Kazan than those in Moscow (26.7%). Some citizens of Kazan combine different means of water purification (0.8%) (Fig. 2.2).

The results of our research survey provided the following data. In Moscow, 15.5% of the respondents indicated that the quality of tap water had improved over the past five years, while the majority (65%) did not notice any changes in it. More than half of the surveyed citizens of Kazan stated that the quality of

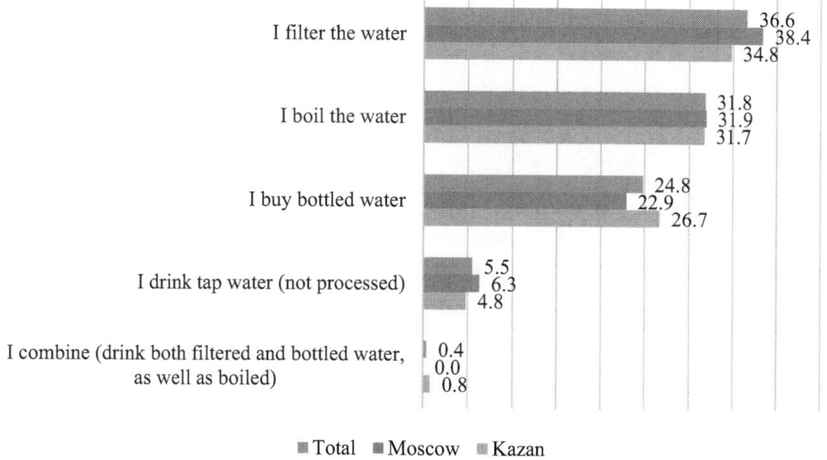

Fig. 2.2. Practices of Citizens to Clean the Tap Water (%).

tap water in their city had not changed over the past five years in their opinion (53.6%). One fourth of the respondents (24.4%) believe that the quality of water deteriorated.

The concerns of the local population are justified. In 2016, Moscow was ranked second among large Russian cities according to the amount of wastewater dumped into natural surface water bodies (824.8 million m^3). Overall, there were 59 cases of high and extreme levels of pollution recorded in Moscow in 2016 by Mosvodokanal, Mosvodostok, and Promotkhody (Gosudarstvennyy doklad, 2017). As a result, the quality of potable water in the city is assessed as satisfactory in two cases out of seven according to the information provided by the authorities (WaterMap, 2018).

The situation is slightly better in Kazan according to the official data. In 2016, Kazan was ranked seventh among large Russian cities according to the amount of wastewater dumped into natural surface water bodies (176.7 million m^3) (Gosudarstvennyy doklad, 2017). That year, Vodokanal accounted for the biggest share of pollution (Vodokanal Kazan, 2017). It also accounted for 92% of water withdrawal from underground sources in Kazan (Ministry of Ecology and Natural Resources of the Republic of Tatarstan, 2017).

However, while the experts in the survey noted that there was a positive trend in the quality of the water supply system in Moscow, in Kazan it was either non-existent or negative. By 2016, the share of industrial water utilization reduced significantly, and the high level of water reuse and recycling consolidated in Moscow (the city is ranked fifth according to this indicator in its federal district of 4,077.04 million m^3) (Gosudarstvennyy doklad, 2017)· In the experts' opinion, the changes that have occurred over the past five years are especially noticeable, "I believe that five years ago, everyone was telling jokes about the Moskva river and what could have happened if you had gone for a swim there. Now, people mostly notice that the quality of water in the river has been improving" (a business representative, Moscow)·

As for Kazan, experts state that the quality of water is much better than it used to be 20–25 years ago, "Technologies have changed, and water became better than it used to be in the mid 1980s and at the beginning of 1990s" (a professional environmentalist, Kazan). However, there have been no significant changes over the past five years. By 2016, the volume of daily water consumption for domestic and drinking purposes per capita and the volume of daily consumption of ground water decreased (Gosudarstvennyy doklad, 2017). However, experts indicate that the situation deteriorated in several other aspects in Kazan. It particularly concerns the composition of tap water:

> *If you try to compare the water we have now to what it used to be in the past, it used to be somewhat translucent, now it's yellow, at least here, in Novo-Savinovskiy district, it's Yamashev district.*
> *(a representative of the scientific community, Kazan).*

SPECIAL ASPECTS OF RUSSIAN POLICIES AIMED AT SOLVING WATER QUALITY ISSUES

Experts admit that the composition of tap water contravenes the state standard of potable water in both cities. In Moscow, such contraventions occur due to the poor functioning of water treatment facilities and problems associated with delivering the purified water to consumers. Water is often transported from remote reservoirs, and the majority of urban pipelines and networks are outdated. As a result, purified water passes through rusty pipes and becomes polluted again. This is why experts insist that it is necessary to boil or filter tap water in Moscow before consumption:

> *Water undergoes the required treatment at water purification plants of Vodokanal, but utility networks are extremely outdated. In some districts with old utility networks, tap water is of low quality simply due to the fact that the pipes are rusty. Even if water is properly treated at water purification plants, it does not always reach consumers in such an acceptable condition.*
> *(a representative of the scientific community, Moscow).*

At the same time, experts have ambivalent opinions on using bottled water. According to some of the experts, excessive water distillation deprives it of the trace elements important for human health. Moreover, there have been cases involving the sales of low-quality bottled water in Moscow. For example, in August 2018, M24.ru, an online media platform, published the following inspection report: about 4% of bottled water samples did not meet the microbiological standards, while 5% of the samples did not feature the required physical and chemical properties (Pochti 760 tysyach, 2018).

Experts also state that in Kazan it is very important to purify tap water before consuming it. Nevertheless, their opinions differ when it comes to determining the stages of purification it has to undergo to become suitable for drinking. Environmentalists believe that unfiltered water should not be used for drinking or cooking even after boiling, which is not always necessary since it would be unreasonable to use potable water for all domestic purposes. On the other hand, it is impossible to setup a centralized dual water supply in Kazan right now, “In my opinion, there’s no point in trying to make tap water potable in big cities because it would be very expensive, financially speaking” (a professional environmentalist, Kazan).

Experts with scientific, activist, and business backgrounds, as well as representatives of nonprofit organizations (NPOs) have a different opinion. In their opinion, authorities have to provide citizens with potable water that does not require any additional domestic cleansing:

> *I think that the quality of tap water is rather low since the local population does not dare to drink it; they install filters and go for spring water, which is the most prominent indicator of the poor quality of potable water.*
>
> *(a representative of the scientific community, Kazan).*

In order to accomplish this, firstly, it would require reducing the frequency of dumping industrial waste into the water bodies of the city. Secondly, it is necessary to renovate the system of water purification at water intake facilities because the chlorine treatment utilized there cannot cleanse the water of organic traces and makes it less suitable for use and consumption by people. Thirdly, the problem of degraded urban facility networks used to deliver water to consumers should be eliminated.

According to the experts interviewed during our research, the water supply problems observed in cities should be solved by local authorities. In Moscow, the local government acts as the central agent that solves all water supply issues. The prompt action taken by the local authorities lies at the core of the urban media discourse associated with water that describes numerous local problems as resolved since “the perpetrators have been found and punished.” The media reports numerous occurrences of the initiation of administrative proceedings against industrial enterprises caught polluting the environment (V Moskve priostanovlena, 2018; Min·ekologii Podmoskov’ya, 2017; V Odintsovskom rayone, 2017). The media highlights the benefits of such measures and proves them with statistics. For example, in October 2017, RIAMO published a comparative analysis on how the situation had been changing over the past six months at lake Kiovo in Lobnya, where the water surface was covered with algae (Glubina ozera, 2017). The measures expected to be taken were described in detail. In July 2018, RIAMO announced that the First

Deputy Minister of Housing and Communal Services of the Moscow Region planned to build 109 water purification plants that would provide 94% of the population of the Moscow Region with high-quality potable water (K kontsu 2018 goda, 2018).

In Kazan, the media discourse associated with water is also centered around the "resolved" issues. However, the issues are usually resolved not through prompt action taken by the authorities but through the complex interaction between the disgruntled local population, authorities, environmentalists, and civic activists. The local population is the central drive behind the policies implemented in Kazan. As a rule, the citizens of Kazan proclaim their dissatisfaction with the quality of the tap water in their city which attracts the attention of the services in charge of the problem and gets it solved. For example, on November 2017, a socio-political newspaper called Vechernyaya Kazan reported the "victory" of villagers from Orekhovka, near Kazan, who fought against the illegal discharge of effluents into a local lake by luxurious cottage settlements in Vostochnaya Orekhovka, Centralnaya Orekhovka, Zapadnaya Orekhovka, and Zagorodnyj klub (Serova, 2017). Business Online is a business newspaper that published articles on the "victory" of inhabitants of the Yurtovo settlement in June 2018, who drew the attention of the authorities in charge to the problem of illegal discharge of sewage waters into the Elkhovka river in the Menzelinsky district (V Menzelinskom, 2018), and on the "victory" of the citizens of Naberezhnye Chelny who requested that environmentalists examined the bank of a river onto which a cottage owner discharged sewage water (Sotsseti, 2018).

Despite the fact that the analysis of the media shows successful resolutions of local water supply issues in both cities, experts have different opinions on the policies implemented there. The effectiveness of the policy implemented in Moscow is rated as high: "The urban policy is aimed at this, so I think that everything will be alright" (a male business representative, Moscow);

> *Tremendous efforts have been made in cooperation with Moscow City Council to implement efficient programs in different areas, and it bears fruit when it comes to the quality of potable water.*
> *(a female media representative, Moscow).*

According to the experts, all water supply issues are being currently addressed and treated in Moscow. Water supply networks are being renovated, and water undergoes several stages of purification before reaching consumers. Experts state that this allowed the quality of water to improve significantly over the past few years, even though it goes unnoticed by the majority of citizens.

According to the experts from Kazan, the measures implemented nowadays do not address the objective of improving the quality of the water supply in the city, so it remains the same or deteriorates. Moreover, the political impetus is often voiced by the concerned citizens of Kazan. Thus, the policy implemented nowadays requires serious revision,

> *There should be a goal set, there should be a striving that the republican authorities should be able to implement. It is highly unlikely that they will set such a goal themselves, but it could be done as a result of the pressure of the dissatisfied population.*
> *(a professional environmentalist, Kazan).*

Thus, the results of the study showed that the available data on the state of air in the cities are contradictory; however, together with expert judgments, we can assume a decrease in air quality in the Russian cities. The quality of water supply, including the safety of tap water, in Kazan and especially in Moscow, has significantly improved and is now rated by professionals and local residents as higher than air quality. The problem of air pollution in the Moscow region and Tatarstan causes many conflicts between the population, business, and authorities that come from landfills and incinerators. The reduction of the maximum permissible levels of pollution for a number of components of the state of atmospheric air along with the lack of desire of the authorities and business to invest in a modern less toxic system of waste recycling and the pursuit of eco-activists provide grounds for a pessimistic scenario for the development of air pollution in the future. Problems of water supply less often cause outbreaks of conflict but remain steadily acute in the perceptions of citizens who do not notice the positive dynamics of water quality. From the point of view of experts, the dynamics are not the same in cities. The advancing policy of the Moscow authorities over the past five years, according to experts, has provided a significant improvement in the processes of water intake, purification, and transportation, as well as a noticeable increase in its quality. The policy of the Kazan authorities is more critical, as it does not contribute to improving the quality of water supply in the city. Meanwhile, air and water pollution is directly related to social inequality, since it negatively affects the health of the population, which does not have the financial capacity to move to a more environmentally friendly environment and is not able to resort to household water treatment methods and buying bottled water.

3

PUZZLE 2: SUSTAINABLE TRANSPORT AND MOBILITY

P. Ermolaeva

In this chapter, we will explore the key trends, challenges, and achievements toward sustainability of transport and mobility systems in the post-soviet Russian landscape. The chapter portrays both positive and negative trends in the Russian transport system and its shift toward sustainability, as well as the citizens' attitudes and practices toward sustainable mobility.

SUSTAINABLE TRANSPORT AND MOBILITY IN RUSSIA: TRENDS, CHALLENGES, AND ACHIEVEMENTS

A significant share of atmospheric air pollution in Russia is caused by motor vehicles, which according to World Health Organization data leads to diseases such as stroke, heart disease, lung cancer, and asthma (World Health Organization, 2009). Greenhouse gas emissions from road transport in Russia are growing faster than in any other sector of the economy due to the rapid growth of personal vehicles (Bakirey & Kharitoshkin, 2014). At the same time, on average, it is automobile transport that accounts for about 40% of total emissions of pollutants in Russia and more than 80% in large cities and megacities (Saginova, 2019).

In this regard, the creation of sustainable transport systems is a solution to the problem of energy consumption, greenhouse gas emissions, and pollutants in large Russian cities. Sustainable transport is a transport system that ensures the fulfillment of a socially and economically justified volume of transport without harming human health and the environment, and without violating the rights of present and future generations (Knie & Scherf, 2017). The principle of the sustainable development of transport in the cities implies a reduction in emissions of CO_2, reduction in pollution of air, as well as the creation of a socially equitable transport system and increase of the city's economic potential. Following V. Vuchic, the author of the concept of "transportation for livable cities," we also note an important property of a stable transport system as intermodality, i.e., balanced inclusion of all modes of transport and means of movement in their most rational role functions (Vuchic, 1999).

One of the six priority objectives until 2030 declared in the Transport Strategy of the Russian Federation was the reduction of the negative impact of the transport system on the environment. The mission of the project is to "make urban transport systems in Russia more efficient and convenient for all road users: motorists, public transport passengers, cyclists, and, of course, pedestrians" (Ministry of Transport of the Russian Federation, 2008). If we turn to the official report for 2018 on the implementation of this strategy, then in almost all respects there are positive changes: reducing greenhouse gas emissions, the creation of an integrated traffic management scheme in major Russian metropolitan areas with priority development of public transport, implementing transport system adaptation projects for non-motorized vehicles and for the use of low-carbon vehicles, and so on.

But in reality how sustainable is the transport system in major Russian cities, and what has changed in the last five years in terms of the expert community, the cities, and their inhabitants? How are the problems of sustainable transport systems reflected in the media?

Most experts interviewed noted the significant role of a balanced and safe transport system in ensuring the "sustainability of the city". In this vein, green vehicles operating on alternative energy sources are of particular importance. In addition, the necessary features of a sustainable transport system were identified as connectivity (a developed network of cycling and walking routes) and intermodality (the ability to easily use and combine different ways of moving around the city). According to experts, the need to develop sustainable transport systems is actively promoted by various civic and scientific initiative groups (for example, the Nordic-Russian cooperation project Eco-Mobility, projects for the development of the bicycle movement St. Petersburg Bicycle, Let's bike it! (Moscow), Gorod PRO Foundation (Yekaterinburg), Hello, Bicycle (Novosibirsk)).

In the media, general rhetoric is aimed at moving toward increasing the sustainability of transport through the development of more environmentally friendly and cost-effective technologies, the use of new energy sources, and the spread of unmanned vehicles. It is, first of all, these urban initiatives, such as public transport, piloting and development in major Russian cities, electric buses, electric vehicles, the conversion of public transport to environmental classes "Euro 4," "Euro 5," and as the "Euro 6," the development of cycling, light rail systems, and car sharing.

However, despite the obvious achievements in the development of sustainable transport systems in the country, experts have noted a number of difficulties. The most serious problems, according to experts, are traffic jams and lack of parking spaces caused by the significant increase in the number of private vehicles in the last five years (most of which run on diesel and petrol engines).

> *...in five years there has been an increase in the number of vehicles, somewhere by 10–20%. All over the world, motor transport is the main pollutant of the atmosphere, therefore, the fact that we plant young trees is naturally not compensated for by the huge flow of motor vehicles that move along our street (representative of an* NGO, *male, Moscow).*

Statistics confirm that there has been a significant increase in the number of vehicles in large Russian cities. According to the Moscow Center for Traffic Management, since 2010 in the capital and the region of Moscow, the number of personal cars has grown from 5.7 to 7.7 million (Svirin, 2019). Moreover, these are only those cars that are registered by Muscovites, while on weekdays the number of vehicles in the city increases significantly due to visitors from the regions. About 3.2–3.6 million cars are driven along the streets of the capital every day. On January 1, 2017, the Kazan passenger car fleet read 368.5 thousand units. Kazan is the fifth largest city with a population of one million people (303 cars per 1000 people with an average of 288 per 1000 in Russia as a whole) (Autostat, 2017).

Experts see the main solution to the problems associated with the increase in the number of vehicles as the restriction of the use of private cars in certain areas (city center) and the parallel harmonious development of public transport. The experts often rely on the experience of Western countries:

> *Now all the major cities ban [cars], for example, in Paris in 2020 in the city center cars will not be able to enter, that is, it is*

> *primarily the fight against emissions of internal combustion engines (representative of the academic sector, female, Moscow)*
>
> *Ideally, I would like our city, if it is so committed to European standards, that the city center is pedestrian, or if not pedestrian, then open only to such necessary modes of transport, that is, … cars also have limited passage to the city center (representative of NGO, male, Kazan).*

Thus, experts believe that restricting the entry of cars to the city center should be associated with the development of pedestrian zones and infrastructure for walking around the city. Along with such proposals, according to experts, it is necessary to pay attention to the development of cycling.

One of the important requirements for a sustainable transport system is environmental friendliness. However, experts note that the transition to environmentally friendly fuel in modern Russian cities is in its infancy. The main strategies in this regard are switching public transport to gas fuel and developing personal and public electric transport. At the same time, the proposed action related to the transition to gas fuel is more popular and widely discussed:

> *…just in the mid-90s, such a program was created specifically for switching to gas fuel, etc. The law has been developed and now it is in existence, for six years it already lies in the State Council – neither here nor there. From this it is already clear that work in this direction is not enough (representative of the academic sector, male, Kazan).*

Indeed, gas, compared to diesel and gasoline, causes significantly lower environmental damage. For example, automobiles using liquefied natural gas emit 90–97% less CO, 25% less CO_2, 35–60% less nitrogen oxides, and at least 50–75% less other non-methane hydrocarbon emissions (Abdrahimova & Safarov, 2018). In addition, due to the relatively simple composition of natural gas compared to traditional motor fuels, there are less emissions of toxic and carcinogenic substances, and there are practically no emissions of particulate matter.

The media discourse suggested that the development of gas-fueled cars would have a greater positive effect on the economy and ecology of Russia than the development of electric vehicles (from the point of view of pro-government media). This is due to the fact that environmentally harmful coal generation remains a source of energy for electric vehicles, and there is also an unresolved issue of the safety of production and disposal of electric motor components. At the same time, the main barrier to the mass transfer of public transport to gas remains its high cost, the lack of gas stations, and insufficient bunkering bases in ports. According to media reports, about 8% of buses (70,000) in Russia operate on gas engine fuel; in cities, the share of such buses is 28%.

Nevertheless, many experts interviewed as part of our study doubt the environmental friendliness of natural gas vehicle (NGV) fuel, as when gas is burned, steam is generated that enhances the greenhouse effect:

> *…as for environmental fuels, now many buses 'feed' on natural gas. This is reasonable, but we must bear in mind the fact that no matter what fuel we burn, in any case it is a hydrocarbon. These are CO_2 and H_2O and, in any case, steam. Recently, everyone has forgotten about the greenhouse effect. With an excess of water gas, there can also be changes in terms of the greenhouse effect (representative of the state administration, male, Moscow);*

"we consider this [gas] an environmentally friendly mode of transport. In fact, gas is also emissions, it is carbon" (representative of the academic sector, male, Kazan).

According to experts, electric transport could become an *appropriate* solution from the point of view of reducing the environmental burden:

> *…[it is necessary] to increase the share of buses on electricity. Not even gas, because gas is also harmful … That is, switching to electric transport, electric cars, railway transport, railway electric transport (representative of the academic sector, male, Kazan).*

The development of electric vehicles (electric buses and electric cars) in Russian cities is the most covered topic in the media among topics of sustainable transport. According to the analytical agency "AUTOSTAT", for 2019 in Russia, 353 electric vehicles have been sold in that time, in contrast to the sale of 144 in 2018 (Autostat, 2017). Since the beginning of the year, over 20 electric charging stations for vehicles have appeared in the Moscow region. The media widely discussed the initiative to provide free parking and reduce taxes on eco-transport:

> *Today we must understand that motorists in hybrid and electric cars are, in fact, donors to the environmental well-being of cities, where cars produce up to 90% of air pollution.*
>
> *(Glava Minprirody predlozhil, 2017).*

Electric buses were first launched in Moscow on September 1, 2018 and in Kazan in November 2018. The media discourse focuses on the advantages of electric buses for Russian cities, their criticism, and test drives by journalists and bloggers. It is noted that, unlike a trolley bus, electric buses consume less electricity, they are silent, suitable for people with disabilities (low floor, there are ramps), there is free Wi-Fi in the cabin, there are smoke and temperature sensors, panic buttons, and a video surveillance system.

In fact, not everything is so rosy – electric buses often break down, do not come on schedule, air conditioners do not work, etc. The media also covers issues such as the development of charging infrastructure for electric vehicles, taking into account the large distances in Russia, and the cold climate. On the one hand, the electric bus fleet is growing in large Russian cities; on the other, there is a tendency to reduce the fleet and routes of trams and trolley buses:

> *...the tram is being revived around the world as a mode of transport ... Against this background, the tram disappears as a mode of transport, it is demolished, they say that it is inconvenient ... (representative of the academic sector, female, Kazan).*

It is also worth noting that some experts doubt the environmental friendliness of electric transport as a large amount of electricity is needed for its operation, produced by city thermal power plants, which, without proper environmental measures, can cause serious harm to the environment. Experts consider that in connection with this, there is an urgent need for the development of alternative energy sources.

> *Environmentally friendly transport that runs on electric traction, it is conditionally clean, because it draws energy from the CHP, and the CHP is located in the city territory, so even if we made electric transport and so on, it's all the same, its level of environmental friendliness will depend on the environmental measures of gas purification at our thermal power plant (representative of an NGO, male, Kazan);*

"and the use of other renewable energy sources, for example, obtaining electricity through solar panels is possible, but so far they are very expensive" (representative of the state administration, male, Kazan).

Experts noted some similar trends regarding the development of transport systems in Moscow and Kazan. Thus, experts point out that motor transport is still environmentally unfriendly and makes a major contribution to air pollution, and there has been a reduction in the fleet and routes of public ground electric transport (mainly trams in Kazan, trolleybuses in Moscow).

Also, in both cities, problem points were identified associated with the development of cycling and walking routes, and most often experts noted their incoherence and the consequent unsuitability for traveling over long distances. At the same time, over the past five years Moscow has moved more toward the establishment of a sustainable transport system: experts note the well-functioning work of public transport, the planned launch of electric buses, the start of sales of electric vehicles, and the gradual development of the necessary infrastructure, as well as the active penetration of new technologies (for example, the development of car sharing). In Kazan, positive dynamics were noted by experts regarding the development of the subway.

SUSTAINABLE MOBILITY: CITIZENS' ATTITUDES AND PRACTICES

Sustainable mobility is defined as the ability to meet the needs of the population in free movement. This category includes time spent on moving around the city, the possibility of saving individual and city resources, caring for health, predictability and the ability to plan movement and environmental impact (Van Wee & Handy, 2016). The most successful actions to improve the mobility of the population in major cities around the world include the development and modernization of public transport systems, enabling ground bus, railway, underground, and suburban transport; the introduction of dedicated lanes on the roads for public transport; improving the comfort and quality of service in public transport; the presence of transport systems of express delivery from the city center to airports; and the creation of a modern transitional and bicycle infrastructure.

To assess the transport infrastructure in the cities of Moscow and Kazan, including environmental modes of transport, citizens were asked to evaluate its different characteristics by completing a survey (Fig. 3.1). The lowest indicators were given to the presence of ecological transport – electric cars, hybrid cars, car sharing (2,3), the availability of parking lots (2,8), the presence of bicycle paths (3,0). A slightly better situation is with transport security (3,4), waiting for transport at bus stops (3,5), quality of the roads in the city (3,5).

Sustainable mobility is associated with discouraging the purchase of a personal car and stimulating the development of urban public transport services. The survey data gathered during our research show that slightly less than half the residents of Kazan and Moscow (47.6%) use a car, and among those who do not use cars more are Muscovites (56%). The latest data correlate with statistics – that between 2010 and 2018 the number of public

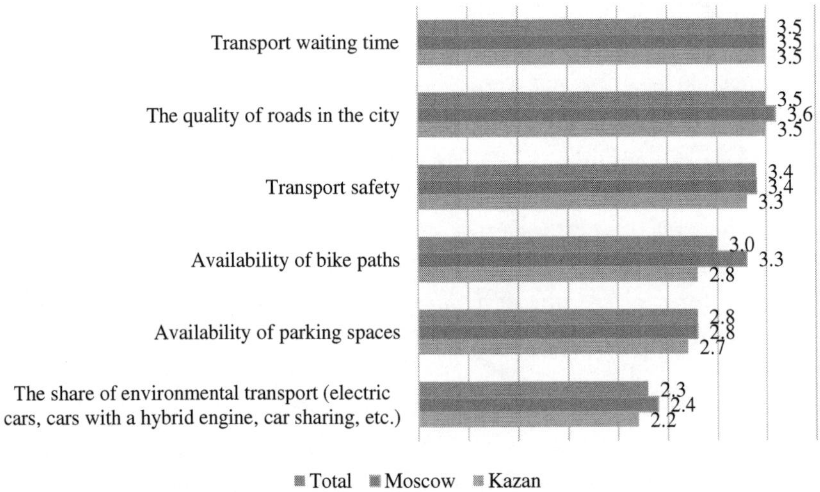

Fig. 3.1. Citizens' Assessments of Different Features of the Transport System in Russian Megacities (Average Points, Where "5" – Excellent, "3" – Moderate, and "1" – Not Satisfactory).

transport passengers in Moscow increased by 460 million people (or 9%) (Moscow Mayor Official website, 2019a).

Data from a nationwide poll in 2019 showed that about one-third of Russians use public transport and travel on it every day (30%), while 18% use it several times a week, and 16% a couple of times a month. In terms of mode of transport, 28% of Russians prefer the bus and 26% the subway. Also, Russians were asked about the reasons for choosing public transport; these were given to be the low cost (43%) or a transfer from a personal car to a public one in order to save time (28%).

Experts interviewed in our research study drew attention to the fact that pricing is extremely important to attract citizens to public transport. Public transport should be affordable from the financial point of view to most citizens from different social strata:

> *...but the fact is that the price of the fare is quite important – especially students suffer from this, those who have small incomes … We need to make public transport more accessible. The policy should be aimed at attracting citizens to a greater use of public transport than personal transport (representative of an NGO, woman, Moscow).*

The need to reduce fares is also confirmed in the data of all Russian sociological surveys. According to the Fund of Public Opinion study conducted in April 2016, 40% of residents of cities with a million-plus populations (except Moscow) consider the amount that they have to spend on public transport to be significant, while only 37% consider it insignificant (Public Opinion Foundation, 2016).

An important opinion was also expressed by the experts that in order to reduce the share of personal vehicles, it is necessary to mount a publicity campaign and communicate with the population, as contradictions are observed in the public mind:

> *...that is, transport in general, it seems to pollute, they understand that it affects their health, but [they think]: my car should be next to me, and I should drive it everywhere, everywhere park, so I can be comfortable (representative of academic sector, male, Moscow).*

Muscovites when traveling by car take an average journey time of an hour at a time to the city, while in Kazan the journey time is up to 30 minutes.

> *Moscow is consistently ranked in the top 10 cities in the world by the number of hours lost in traffic jams. In 2016, in Moscow it was possible to stand in traffic jams for an average of 91 hours over a period of 240 days, which is second only to Los Angeles with 104 hours globally (representative of the analytical center, woman, Moscow).*

In recent years, the practice of cycling in large Russian cities is actively developing. The civil society has taken the main role in promoting this process. Activists of bicycle communities organize large-scale joint events, conduct educational activities, broadcast a cycle culture to the townspeople, and hold discussions with authorities on the creation of infrastructure for the development of cycling in cities. According to Greenpeace, about 230 km of bike lanes and paths have now been built in Moscow (90 km on the road network and 140 km in parks); however, there are only about 1,867 parking lots and 430 bike rental stations (Ivannikova, 2018). In 2013, in Kazan, thanks to the preparation for the Universiade of students, a public bike rental system appeared in the city before other Russian cities, with a total length of the bike paths of 4.8 km (P.Ermolaeva, 2014; Kuznetsova, 2013). An example for other Russian cities is the city of Almetyevsk, which is located in the Republic of Tatarstan, for which the Danish bureau Copenhagenize Design Company planned the bicycle infrastructure. Before the start of the bicycle program, there was only 4 km of bike paths in the city, of which 3.1 km were in parks. In 2016, another 50 km of bike paths connected into a single network were built, and parking lots appeared at the "attraction points." In 2017, the length of the bike paths was increased to 83 km, and by 2020, it is planned to expand the network to 200 km. The bicycle infrastructure in Almetyevsk is being developed on the initiative of the city administration, but at the same time they are consulting the townspeople: the results of opinion polls provide the basis for decisions.

These trends have been positively evaluated by the media and the experts in our survey. However, the experts noted that a safe infrastructure and communication routes have not yet been created in Russian cities. There are also "cultural" problems such as motorists parking their cars on pedestrian streets. "Now there is an idea to build a bike path around Lake Sredny Kaban" (Kazan author's note).

> *It's a good idea, there's a nice landscape, everything is beautiful and very nice ... It doesn't solve the problem of reducing the traffic load in the city center ... But I would like it to be a solution that would be connected with the infrastructure and reducing the anthropogenic load of transport (representative of the academic sector, woman, Kazan).*

The survey in our research showed that on an ongoing basis, about 20% of people in Moscow and Kazan use their bicycles. Among the main reasons for not using a bicycle/scooter were the following: the habit of using public transport (28%), there is no interest in cycling as an element of leisure (25%), unsafe (22%), poor climatic conditions (20%), health does not allow (18%), the small number of bike paths (17%), there are no facilities for parking a bicycle (15%). For residents of the Russian capital, Moscow, the obstacle hindering people from cycling is the habit of using public transport (37%), while people in Kazan are much more likely than Muscovites to have a lack of interest in this type of leisure activity (29%) (Fig. 3.2).

The prevailing climate in both cities of Moscow and Kazan of a long winter period with low temperatures and high rainfall is an obstacle to the use of a bicycle and also places high demands on the quality of the bicycle infrastructure and its level of service. In addition, as in many transition economies, in Russia, a car carries not only comfort and speed but also social status and is a symbol of the success of its owner (Saginova & Zavyalova, 2018).

The joint consumption economy is becoming popular among Russians in which car sharing is one of the key sectors of the new economic model. Currently, there are 26 operators in 15 cities in the car sharing market in Russia; 17 operators (65% of companies) are concentrated in Moscow, where the maximum demand for the service is also observed. The process is actively

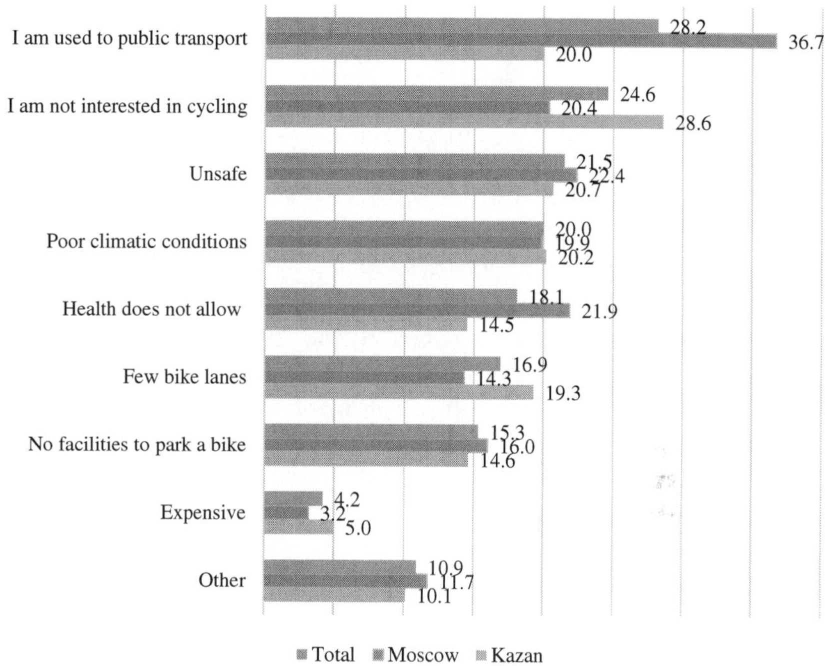

Fig. 3.2. The Main Reasons for Not Using a Bike/Scooter (%).

supported by the mayor's office in Moscow, in the first place, through subsidizing parking.

For car sharing users, 35% of city dwellers use different degrees of periodicity. The main users of car sharing in Russia are young people aged 21–35, making 7–19 trips a month in cars of two to five car sharing companies and spending 1,942–4,617 rubles on trips (Ivanova & Lyubimova, 2019).

> *Until 2025, the market for shared urban transport will more than double and reach 1.6 trillion rubles. At the same time, an increase of 377 billion rubles will occur due to the replacement of public transport, and of 474 billion rubles due to the crowding out of personal cars (representative of an analytical agency, woman, Moscow).*

At the same time, experts identify a number of difficulties in the implementation of the car sharing institution in Russia, among which we can single out such factors as the lack of legislation regulating relations arising in the provision of this service and the risk of getting a damaged car, the problems in online applications. In addition, car sharing rates in Russia are currently quite high, which, together with the lack of cars within walking distance, makes this service less attractive than using a taxi.

The chapter shows that the initiatives of city authorities in the field of sustainable transport and mobility development include the development of public transport, car sharing, bicycle routes, and light rail systems. However, there are a number of unresolved problems that are exacerbated by the constant increase in the number of personal vehicles. These include the use by city residents mainly of personal vehicles, the imperfections of the public transport system, the serious environmental burden due to the use of vehicles with gasoline and diesel engines, the low level of development of alternative modes of transport, and the inconvenience and insecurity of bike and foot routes. The main strategies for improving the environmental friendliness of the movement are switching public transport to gas fuel and developing personal and public electric transport.

4

PUZZLE 3: ENERGY EFFICIENCY AND ENERGY CONSUMPTION

Y. Ermolaeva

The chapter describes the structure of the Russian energy system, including the specifics of establishing a sustainable energy policy in Russian cities according to the opinions of different local stakeholders, the key areas of such a policy, and the contribution made by the resource-efficient practices respected by the citizens.

FEATURES OF THE RUSSIAN ENERGY SYSTEM AND ITS DEVELOPMENT PROSPECTS

Russia is the largest country in the world, and it has a disproportionately large share (up to 15% of the world reserves) of proven fossil fuel reserves (Ministry of Energy of the Russian Federation, 2018). Russia is responsible for over 10% of the global production and over 20% of the export of crude energy (Ministry of Energy of the Russian Federation, n.d.). Russian fuel and energy complex was the largest producer of energy resources in the USSR and their second-largest consumer in the world. In 2008 and 2012, it went through recession but stayed afloat despite the world crisis thanks to its technological stability. This stability was formed against the backdrop of certain conditions and under the influence of these challenges:

(1) *Climatic and natural specifics increasing energy consumption.* Russia's cold climate increases the share of energy used for electricity and heating by 20% and elevates the costs of construction and maintenance

of residential and production facilities (Ministry of Energy of the Russian Federation, 2016). Russia's actual energy consumption is the fourth largest in the world, after China, the USA, and India. In 2018, it comprised 1,076.2 billion kWh. The climatic conditions obstruct the utilization of such renewable energy sources as solar energy and biomass in Russia. These factors shape the main challenge of the Russian energy sector, the high energy intensity that signifies consuming a large amount of energy and fuel to maintain the primary and secondary processes of production, operation, and service provision based on the given technological system, which increases the negative impact of the energy sector on the environment (Barinova, Laitner, & Lanshina, 2016).

(2) *The inequality in distributing energy resources is compensated by an enhanced system of centralized energy communication.* Only 18% of Russian regions have their own energy sources, while others have to transport them from hundreds and thousands of kilometers away (Ministry of Energy of the Russian Federation, 2018). At the same time, regions' problems associated with the eco-friendly modernization differ depending on the unequal natural, economic, and cultural capital.

(3) *The global trend toward green energy and the dependency of the country's economy on the energy sector forced Russia to modify its energy sector to be more eco-friendly* (IAEA, 2019; Ministry of Energy of the Russian Federation, 2018). According to the Paris Agreement and sustainable development goals, by 2030, Russia has to reduce its greenhouse gas emissions by 25–30% compared to the level of 1990. This limits the admissible volume of emissions to 150,000 tons of CO_2 equivalent, and if the quotas are exceeded, since 2025, enterprises will have to pay a carbon tax (United Nations, 2015b). Changing the strategy led to the appearance of two opposing ideologies of "green" and "brown" economy (Andreenko et al., 2015).

These challenges motivated the government to shift from the raw-materials export model of development to the strategy of a "stimulating infrastructure" that was believed to go through at least three stages from 2014 to 2035 (Marchenko & Solomin, 2015).

The first two stages are meant to change the management system of the fuel sector before 2026 and to achieve maximum energy efficiency in the gas sector (Varol, 2013). During the third stage, after 2026, the country is supposed to shift to the "energy system of the new generation, to begin using the traditional renewable energy sources with high efficiency, and to develop smart energy systems" (Kopylov, 2015).

The fourth stage (2036–2050) is theoretically determined as a projected alternative of the technological development where the dependency on carbon energy resources is minimized or eliminated. The energy strategy lists the nuclear energy and large-scale hydraulic power industry as an alternative allowing to reduce oil extraction and exports and to improve the energy affordability indexes in Russian regions; the potential of small-scale renewable sources is the last one to be considered (Bushuyev, Makarov, & Mastepanov, 2010).

Energy Market Economics in Russia. Governmental and municipal establishments are being stimulated to make agreements with energy providers, target performance indicators are being established, and cost-saving objectives aim at the modernization of different industrial and energy sectors (Lunden, Fjaertoft, Overland, & Prachakova, 2013). Energy efficiency management systems based on ISO 50001 are being created, thanks to which many enterprises can reduce their energy consumption by 10–15%.

Russia's energy market is predominantly represented by oil and gas corporations of the national and federal scale. Russia's green energy market functions according to the closed-loop principle, where all market components (equipment manufacturing, development, operation) are gathered within one group of companies, which helps to lower the risks of entering a new market. Several investment funds (e.g., Falcon Capital, Bright Capital) and international energy companies (e.g., Enel, E.On, Fortum) show interest in Russia's wind energy sector. As for the small-scale hydraulic power industry, OAO RusHydro is the absolute leader. There isn't a single governmental program aimed at supporting the development of biogas technologies, despite the fact that Russia possesses 25% of the world's wood supply. For the Russian economy, the cumulative effect of developing renewable sources of energy will comprise 200 million rubles before 2025, while the total annual positive effect will amount to 68 billion rubles without considering the expenditures associated with the environmental protection and public health preservation. Besides, it will be possible to reduce the cost of environmental measures intended for pollution abatement by 18.5 billion rubles and to redistribute the budget according to other priorities of the environmental policy. Over this period of time, it is planned to create approximately 100,000 new workplaces in the sector, even though, given the number of 1.98 million employees of the energy sector, this figure is insignificant (Lough, 2011).

TRADITIONAL AND RENEWABLE ENERGIES IN RUSSIA

The sectors of fossil energy and renewable energy function within a single system featuring centralized management. The energy system consists of seven federal regional energy systems united into one (Energy Research Institute, 2014; Morarjee, 2010). Departments and ministries develop local programs, while governmental and non-profit agencies test these programs and evaluate projects.

Profit organizations draw analytical reports and regulate the private market; scientific establishments create and promote their solutions. Systemic enterprises create sub-institutions according to energy sectors and supply energy. Russian economists and power engineers use such terms as "energy efficiency," "energy intensity," and "emissions per unit of energy generated" (Kopylov, 2015).

The potential of renewables in Russia is huge but barely fulfilled. In 2012, only 4% of the country's energy supply was coming from renewable energy sources, two-thirds of which were supplied by the hydraulic power industry. Meanwhile, the economic potential of Russian renewable energy sources is colossal and by some estimates comprises 270 million tons of standard fuel per year, where 115 million tons of standard fuel per year is attributed to the geothermal energy, 65.2 million tons of standard fuel per year comes from small-scale hydroelectric power plants, 35 million tons of standard fuel per year is supplied by the biomass, 12.5 million tons of standard fuel per year is sourced by the solar power, 10 million tons of standard fuel per year could be delivered by the wind energy, and 36 million tons of standard fuel per year originates from low-grade heat sources (Bushuyev, 2014). As for the factors impeding the development of renewable energy sources in Russia, they are the availability of a heavy supply of fossil fuel and the existence of an infrastructure servicing it, as well as lack of government incentives for the sector (Merle-Beral, 2005).

However, there are several renewable energy programs being deployed. In 2019, Pyat' Gigavatt program aimed at developing solar and wind energy until the year 2024 was approved of. It is envisioned that by 2024, the electric power output of solar and wind stations will comprise approximately 1% of the total energy production. It is commercially viable to install geothermal power stations in West Siberia, while seacoasts and islands of the Arctic Ocean are suitable for wind energy (Kostomarova & Blake, 2009).

Energy Priorities of Russian cities. The possibilities of employing the green energy in existing cities are limited due to the high urban density, which is why its alternative usages for cities are being discussed.

According to the Science and Technological Directions forecast (Ministry of Energy of the Russian Federation, n.d.), until the year 2035, when it comes to the deployment of the Russian fuel and energy complex in cities, the primary emphasis is placed upon ensuring the conservation of energy, utilizing energy-efficient materials for construction, employing smart metering devices and energy-efficient lighting systems based on fluorescent and LED devices. According to reports, the usage of renewable energy sources in Moscow and its region has been depleted (Ermolenko, Proskuryakova, & Ermolenko, 2017; Ratner & Nizhegorodtsev, 2017). In cities, waste incineration plants deducing energy and the incineration of remaining residuary waters are used as renewables.

While most cities are energy-excessive (produce more energy than necessary), regions often experience power shortages (there is no centralized energy supply) due to the existence of isolated settlements featuring boiler facilities operating through using traditional sources of energy. More than half of the fuel sector of Russian cities is presented by gas and coal generation, which provokes greenhouse gas emissions. This, the potential of hydropower stations, is employed at the periphery of Moscow and the Moscow region. Solar and wind generations lack capacity, and there are individual low-capacity solar panels installed in the city. Overall, the share of RES in the total power balance of Moscow amounts to 0.07% (Ministry of Energy of the Russian Federation, n.d.).

EXPERT ASSESSMENT OF DEVELOPING SUSTAINABLE ENERGY IN RUSSIA

Russia's energy strategy cannot be labeled as a simple transition from fossil energy to green energy. The infrastructural change implies the transformation of a unitary energy system and serving the interests and capacities of the traditional and renewable energy lobbies.

Experts believe that the concept of green energy includes these characteristics: (1) providing for the energy needs of a city while avoiding energy-excessiveness, (2) continuity, (3) employing a share of renewable energy sources or environmentally-oriented energy generation sources with due regard to minimizing emissions, (4) an energy-saving and energy-efficient apparatus, (5) minimization of the negative impact on the climate, (6) the energy sector provides eco-friendly fuel for transportation, (7) secure energy-efficient equipment, (8) adoption of the energy-saving culture by the population. In expert opinion, the energy-efficient and energy-saving policy does not comply with the sustainable energy concept as of now but is striving for that.

Experts have laid out an *optimistic* and a *pessimistic* forecast for developing sustainable energy in cities. The *optimistic* forecast is associated with increasing the share of utilized smart technologies, substituting the old equipment of gas stations with more energy-efficient machinery, promoting the culture of using energy-saving domestic appliances and lighting equipment, improving the energy efficiency standards of buildings under construction, and automation of the energy calculation.

The *pessimistic* forecast is related to the fact that "systematic decisions addressing the problems of water and energy supply are not being made, and the development of independent municipalities is being severely obstructed" (a representative of the public administration of Moscow); besides, the bureaucratic apparatus of the housing and utility sector is poorly regulated, which affects the development of the technologies mentioned in the optimistic forecast, which could cause stagnation.

Conservation of Energy and Energy Efficiency in Cities. When it comes to cities, experts noted positive dynamics associated with the increase of housing facilities and a proportionally developing energy sector over the given time, as well as with applying international standards in energy efficiency. Citizens used counters to control their water and energy consumption on their own. Heat supply and transfer have been improved depending on the temperature conditions. Experts believe that coal and gas generation will grow, despite the principles of sustainable urban development since there are no other effective alternatives at the moment. The largest energy loss occurs through the enclosing structures in buildings and insulated pipes. As for the residential and business sector, most buildings remain energy-inefficient since significant heat losses lead to the overconsumption of energy, "it is necessary to change a lot of things in the management of the housing and utility sector so that the expenditures are under control" (a representative of the public administration of Kazan). Experts also recommended avoiding spending extra money on decorating the city center. But experts positively assessed new buildings according to the employment of energy-efficient technologies.

Renewables. Currently, there is no independent RES program in macroregions, and the renewables are viewed as one of the supplementary measures of the general energy conservation strategy. Experts singled out several groups of *stakeholders* interested in the development of RES in macroregions. (1) Independent corporations producing equipment. Their point of interest is the autonomous provision of consumers with energy within their individual households and the installation of the energy-saving equipment based on RES in multistorey buildings; (2) The scientific community collaborating with enterprises; (3) citizens as independent energy consumers.

Experts believe that the *economic regulation* of RES should be increased. Measures will be implemented by introducing changes to the energy-balance carriers (for example, if the volume of waste increases, the volume of secondary resources (waste) for the energy generation will also increase) and distributing the economic investments accordingly.

Experts were also asked to answer several questions related to developing RES in cities with limited capacities.

Although the potential of hydropower plants is fully realized in Moscow, there are large stations designed for the incineration of the wastewater sludge and waste incineration plants with a total capacity of 26 MW; experts are skeptical about applying RES within the megalopolis since it is impossible to ensure the industrial-scale provision of RES with the energy of the city. As for the types of RES, "solar power panels are preferable for Moscow" (an energy engineer, male).

According to experts, implementing RES in Kazan is "at a low, rudimentary level", despite the high potential of installing small-scale hydropower plants and sun generators in the region and in the Republic of Tatarstan. The interest in employing RES in construction and low-grade heat sources is also growing. Overall, experts noted the serious restriction that exists in Kazan and other cities in general,

> *Cities cannot exist by means of the sun and wind, the energy consumption is too big there. RES are great for the areas featuring low energy needs and small capacities that have backup power systems in addition (a representative of the energy sector, Moscow).*

MEDIA DISCOURSE ON "BROWN" AND "GREEN" ECONOMY MODELS

The specifics of the energy discourse in the Russian media are the following:

(1) Looking forward to the future developments in energy conservation and energy efficiency within the scope of the traditional energy system

on the one hand and striving to set the course toward sustainable and renewable energy on the other. An interview of the Russian President, representatives of the Ministry of Energy, and Herman Gref, economist and CEO of Sberbank, offers an anticipated forecast for developing the energy sector. It is expected that by 2040, the extraction of gas and oil will slightly decrease by the estimate of 10–15% (Gref, 2020). This niche will be occupied by renewable sources of energy. The media considers the development of RES in Russia to be slow. By various estimates, it does not cover 50–70% of Russia's territory with a population of 20 million people. But the renewables can solve the issue of energy accessibility for the individual households excluded from the central energy system (Semashko, 2018). RES are considered an additional developing energy generation sector by the media, experts, and the development program. The media sheds light upon the RES development measures implemented by such governmental institutions as the Ministry of Energy, Ministry of Economic Development, Ministry of Industry and Trade, and the Federal Antimonopoly Service (FAS) to support the generation of energy based on RES after 2024. According to the media discourse, the key player supporting the development of RES in Russia is Anatoly Chubais (CEO of the Russian Nanotechnology Corporation that belongs to the state). According to Chubais, the volume of the domestic solar generation market amounts to 1.76 gigawatt (GW), that of wind generation reaches 3.28 GW, while the MSW reclamation market is equal to 0.445 GW (Gref, 2020).

(2) Export-oriented geopolitics (energy sector to establish new economic connections both in the traditional and RES sectors) (Dolya energoresursov, 2017). The media offers a justification for developing a raw-materials export model for Russia, given the dependency of its economic welfare on the export of oil and gas. Alexei Teksler, Governor of the Chelyabinsk region and a legislative drafter, announced that the energy balance of Russia is one of the cleanest in the world. "The share of coal comprises only 15% of our country's energy balance, while this indicator exceeds 65% in China, almost reaches 30% in Europe, and slightly exceeds 30% in the USA. 50% of Russia's energy balance is covered by gas, which is two times eco-friendlier than coal and 1.5 times eco-friendlier than black oil fuel," the first deputy head of the energy department stated (Vazhny tekhnologicheskie, 2017).

Once again, renewable energy measures are viewed as supplemental. According to RBC, a new high-tech economic sector reaching 1 trillion rubles in volume, or 0.1% of GDP, will form in Russia, and RES solutions for export are believed to be a promising area of focus, as well as the export of energy obtained through RES. There is also a large industrial cluster featuring a potential that could be realized at export markets and in Russian R&D.

(3) The media discourse focusing on the promising trends in traditional and renewable energy is combined with the topic of smart technologies and intellectual networks of urban development.

Urban territories with a developed energy infrastructure cannot transition to RES. According to the references on media portals, Rosatom and Rosseti propose the most promising solutions and are the most influential in the energy sector. Rosatom's key focus areas include artificial intelligence and other digital solutions for the industry and service applications, renewable and smart energy, 3D printing and new materials, and systems of smart and energy-efficient urban development.

The media covers "Copenhagenization" as a strategy of modern urban development in Russia that implies the development of alternative means of transportation and the state promotion of urban cycling, car-sharing networks, bike sharing, carpooling services, and the concept of a post-carbon city, according to which the cities of tomorrow are the ones featuring the most political, economic, and cultural impact on the world rather than the most innovative ones (Mironov, 2018). The environmental strategy of such a city implies reducing the consumption of energy resources when producing heat and electric energy, reducing emissions, raising awareness among the population, and incentivizing the transition to electric cars.

Energy priorities affect the development of public transportation, where the priority is given to electric transport. In 2019, the first electric bus was launched in Moscow.

> *Thanks to the new energy-efficient model of urban development in Moscow, it became possible to reduce harmful emissions into the atmosphere by 33%, reduce the consumption of gas by 20% and the consumption of heat by 6.2%, despite the large scale of constructions.*
>
> *(Ministry of Energy of the Russian Federation, n.d.).*

ENERGY AND WATER SAVING PRACTICES AMONG RUSSIANS

Energy- and water-saving in residential buildings are regulated by laws and regulations. In Russia, the consumption of resources can be controlled at two levels, those are metering the consumption for a whole building thanks to apartment block metering units and metering the consumption for an individual apartment thanks to apartment-level metering units. This allows us to employ consumption-based billing and to determine the share of each consumer in the building when paying for the resources. Sometimes, it is impossible to install such metering units (in houses built before 2000) due to the constructional features of heating systems and wear-and-tear of in-house networks.

Approximately 57% of Russians carefully monitor their consumption of energy resources and strive to economize it. The number of respondents who do this to save natural resources increased fivefold over a period of four years (from 3% in 2015 to 15% in 2019) (Ministry of Natural Resources and Environment of the Russian Federation, 2017b). 29% of those who do not monitor their consumption of energy resources believe that they "already adhere to the principles of responsible consumption and only consume as much as they need." Every fifth respondent (22%) admitted being unable to be economical. Approximately 12% of the surveyed state there is no need to save energy resources. 5% of Russians simply forget to do it (VCIOM: bol'she poloviny, 2019).

One-third of the respondents have been participating in the annual Earth Hour event since 2015, and their number has been increasing annually. Now it comprises 56% (VCIOM: Za energopotrebleniem, 2019). Compared to 2013, the number of Russians aware of this event increased.

When surveying the citizens of Russian cities, we assessed the housing facilities with an impact on energy conservation and energy- and water-saving practices. We also paid attention to the fit-out of buildings, equipment in use, and energy-saving activities. Russian cities experience no power shortages as 95% of citizens are connected to the central heating system; however, 74% in Moscow and 66% in Kazan cannot regulate the temperature independently, which imposes significant restrictions on the possibility of adhering to energy-saving behaviors. Here, the problem can only be solved by changing the radiators, which will be costly for the residents. This lays the foundation of a certain inequality associated with the ability to save energy, as new energy-efficient buildings outperform older buildings that suffer from energy losses.

Due to the cold climate, residents strive to retain warmth by installing insulated windows, doors, floors, or using heat-insulating materials. Thus, 21% of the respondents look to install insulated windows, 46% set up energy-efficient windows, 27% use light transmission glass, and 11% monitor the lever of illumination. Insulated doors are less popular. Only 16% of the respondents insulate their doors.

Energy-efficient behavior is stimulated by economic incentives and habit. But Russia is ranked 71st according to the cost of electricity. The average cost of electricity in Russia is estimated as 8.20 US cents per kW, or about 2.96 rubles per kW. Russia is ranked 13th in the list of countries of the cheapest average prices of electricity (Ren21, 2011). Thus, 62% of respondents turn off the lights when leaving a room; about a third of the respondents disconnect electric devices from the power source. 40% of the population monitor heat losses, try to close doors and windows when necessary and to monitor the temperature of ACs. Other citizens have no such habit or consider the energy losses insignificant in terms of financial losses.

Almost 91% of respondents have electricity and water meters installed, which allows them to control water suppliers and public utility offices and to avoid paying in case of pipe breaks and water losses in water supply networks. 58% of the population purchase household appliances featuring energy efficiency classes of A and A+. However, digital energy-efficient practices are uncommon among the population, as only 15% have energy-saving mobile apps. Heating control via smartphone is even less popular and is only employed by 4.5% of the population (Fig. 4.1).

According to our survey, 90% of the population have water metering devices. Most respondents use primitive water-saving methods. 67% of the surveyed make sure they turn off the tap when not using water, while 40.8% of the respondents reduce the flow of water from the tap in this case. 44% of citizens take showers instead of baths, and only 14% of the respondents use dishwashers to save water (Fig. 4.2).

There are a number of conditions restricting energy- and water-saving practices that depend on the energy efficiency class of the house itself and on the design of heating appliances. The economic circumstances of establishing a more energy-saving lifestyle and home are yet another restrictive condition. But there are simple universal practices available to everyone, such as monitoring heat and energy losses, closing doors, disconnecting unused devices from the power source, turning off the lights and taps. They are not pervasive, but such practices contribute to the conservation of resources by regulating the primary flows of energy and water.

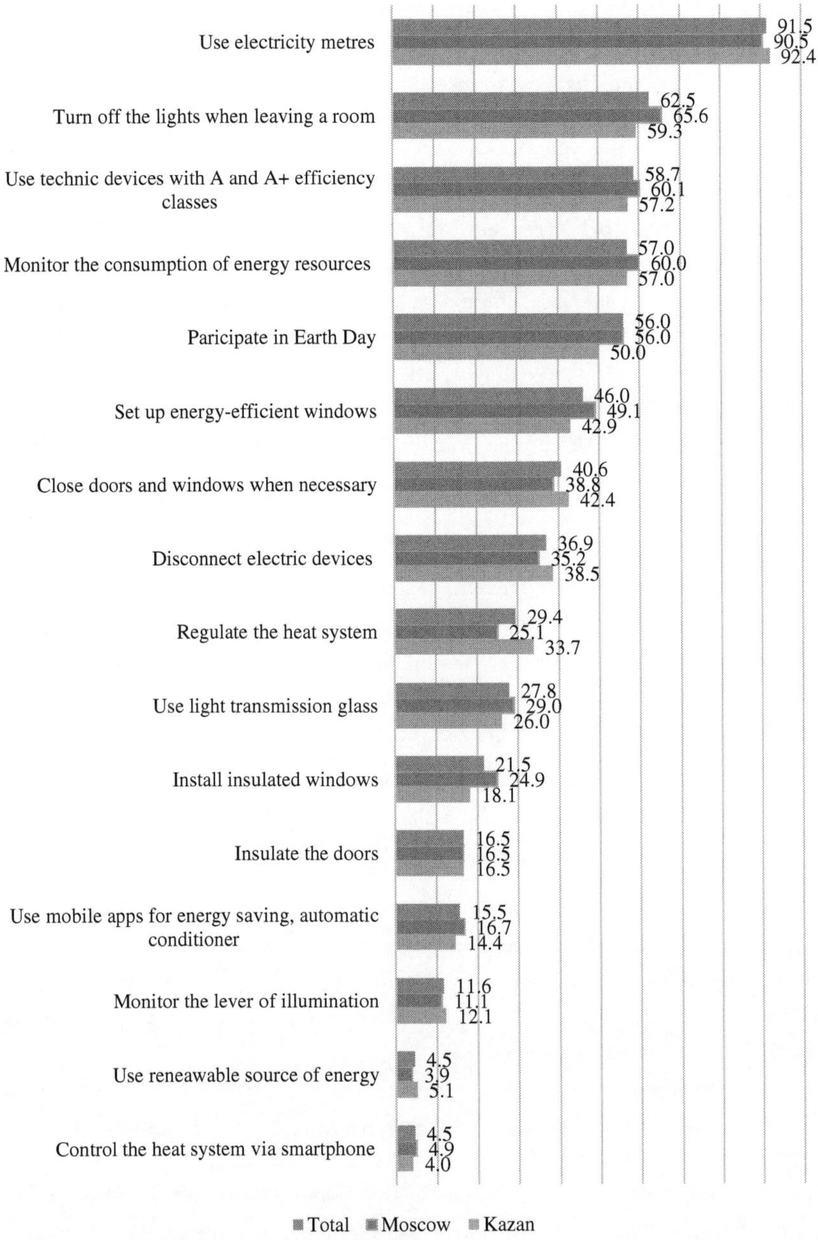

Fig. 4.1. Energy-saving Practices (%).

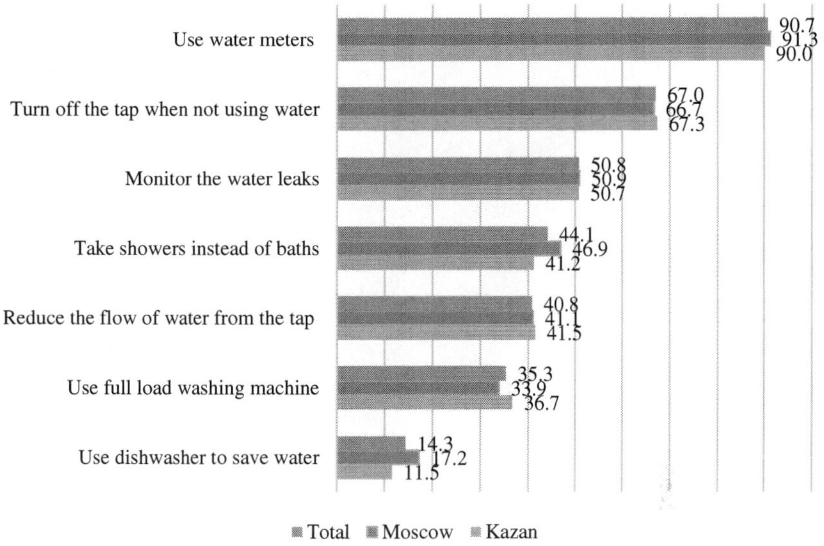

Fig. 4.2. Water-saving Practices (%).

The chapter shows that there are two priorities in the energy program of Russian cities, (1) energy conservation and energy efficiency of the hydrocarbon complex and (2) the gradual increase of the energy obtained from renewable sources. Energy practices became more popular for citizens, people – 60–65% of the population is involved into different resource-saving practices. The centralization and monopolism of the energy structure bears the advantages of continuity and reliability of the power supply utilities but also raises barriers to developing a decentralized renewable energy system that tries to exist within the same unitary system.

5

PUZZLE 4: WASTE MANAGEMENT

Y. Ermolaeva and P. Ermolaeva

In this chapter, we will explore the principles of developing a zero-waste policy in the Russian waste management system and determine the challenges, stakeholders and discourses of waste management in Russia. We will also analyze Russians' practices in managing municipal solid waste and outline the main points of social tension from the perspective of the environmental justice and inequality concept.

MODERN WASTE MANAGEMENT SYSTEM IN RUSSIA: CURRENT STATE, ACHIEVEMENTS, AND CHALLENGES

After the collapse of the USSR, the elements of the circular economy (plastic, metal, and glass recycling plants) were diminished significantly, and local authorities started taking 90% of their waste to landfills. The municipal authorities assumed the responsibility for waste management, and only 5%–7% of waste was recycled (Ermolaeva, 2019a).

Consumption and waste generation rates in modern Russia are similar to those in the economically developed countries of Western Europe and the US (United Nations, 2015a). However, unlike them, Russia does not have a well-developed recycling industry. The life cycle of waste management predominantly reflects the linear economy inherent to developing countries rather than circular. According to the Federal Service for Supervision of Natural Resource Usage, by 2018, 38 billion 73 million tons of industrial and domestic waste, which makes approximately 400 kg per person every year, have been accumulated in Russia (Ministry of Natural Resources and Environment of the Russian Federation, 2018). The amount of generated waste continues to grow. For example, in 2017, it increased by 12.5% compared to the level of 2016 (Ministry of Natural Resources and Environment of the Russian Federation, 2018). Thus, the government faced the need to implement a new zero-waste economy scheme based on the experience of European countries.

The new waste management system only took off in 2014 (Federal'nyj zakon ob othodah, 2020). Then, such terms as "recycling," "regeneration," etc. were introduced into the law, which did not affect the infrastructural development of the industry and was done solely for the international standardization of terms. The program outlined new waste management principles that involved giving the priority to reclamation over waste incineration and landfilling and determined the terms for calculating and paying the environmental charges. The reform was prepared at the higher governmental levels and did not take into consideration any local specifics (Territorial'naya skhema obrashcheniya s othodami, 2016).

Russia combines several management schemes united in a single system and has the following features: (1) centralized waste management (development of a single law that all the regions are supposed to comply with), as well as the distribution of legal responsibilities and assignment of legal functions to different departments (the Ministry of Natural Resources, the Ministry of Industry, the Federal Service for Surveillance on Consumer Rights Protection, the Ministry of Science and Higher Education, and ministries responsible for the different sectors of economy, such as oil industry, metallurgic industry, gas industry, etc.). Departments and ministries are still responsible for individual production and consumption sectors, while not being united into a single functional system with a single waste tracking, reclamation, and liability scheme. (2) The federal waste management system that includes 85 territorial subjects possessing equal rights that can amend the law and develop their own waste management schemes as long as they comply with the main law. However, the density of population, industrial capacities, and the climatic conditions affecting the morphology of waste generation are different in different Russian regions, as well as the reclamation resources, which imposes the need of developing local schemes. Russia is not the only country featuring a federal waste management system. Similar systems were also implemented in the US and Australia, but they featured higher autonomy and fewer responsible parties because they began as local grassroots initiatives, which is why they were more effective (Davies, 2008; Gentil et al., 2010).

The main challenge of developing a zero-waste economy in Russian cities is finding the balance between the centralized and local approach to waste management against the backdrop of regional economic, social, and geographic differences. In 2017, the "Russian Environmental Operator" appeared, similar to the regional operator in Europe (Russian Environmental Operator, https://reo.ru/). The regional operator accumulates all money flows coming from the population, management companies, and other domestic waste generators and makes agreements on factual waste handling with other market actors for the minimal term of 10 years. The new institute regulates the relationships between all sector parties associated with waste management in each region, creation of an infrastructure for waste collection and disposal, as well as the development of necessary sorting capacities. Through this, the Environmental Operator mitigates the flaws of the central element of the waste management system and reinforces the federal system. As of the end of 2017, territorial waste management schemes were enacted in 85 subjects of the Russian Federation, while regional waste management programs were developed in 52 subjects and are still being discussed. A part of the territorial schemes enacted on time were declared invalid and sent for revision (Ministry of Natural Resources and Environment of the Russian Federation, 2018).

The main function of the regional operator is handling household waste; nevertheless, 95% of waste is industrial. The responsibility for the industrial waste used to be distributed among different departments, and the possibility of assigning industrial waste management to the regional operator is being currently discussed in order to shift the centralized management from different structures to a single position which will allow the creation of a "scheme of general waste balance management in the country."

As for the positive tendencies, the electronic base managed by the operator made the objects of the infrastructure transparent. It provided the estimated balance (of material and economic flows) and MSW stream schemes, connecting regional logistics. It is planned to add yet another element widely used in Europe; that is, an extended producer responsibility according to which the producer bears the expenses for the recycling of their products.

Currently, there are a number of systematic challenges in Russia, for some of which solutions are underway.

Challenge 1: Landfills. After separate waste collection is performed, 80%–90% of waste is sent to landfills. By 2018, 4–7 million hectares of land were occupied by landfills, which made these territories unsuitable for the efficient use of natural resources (Ministry of Natural Resources and Environment of the Russian Federation, 2018). Currently, the number of unauthorized dumping sites is rapidly decreasing; old landfills are being shut down, while new landfills are being provided with the systems of wastewater filters and gas extraction for heating purposes (Ob obrashchenii s tverdymi kommunal'nymi otkhodami, 2018). However, landfills are still a problem for cities with a population over 1 million people, especially if they are industrial centers. The stream of generated waste and crowded landfills lead to conflicts between the government as the owner and those who live in the regions and cities where this waste is being stored.

Challenge 2: The expansion of incineration plants, which is the stumbling block to the implementation of the zero-waste strategy. Citizens and experts have major doubts regarding the expediency of the advancement of such a practice in the capacity of the main resource-efficient management strategy (Postanovlenie ob utverzhdenii, 2016). Citizens and experts are either "strongly opposed" to it or find it "acceptable given certain conditions". The second position involves two conditions, such as safety of incineration plants, which was noted by chemists and technologists, and maintaining an acceptable level of resource efficiency, using waste incineration plants as the last technological element in the chain of secondary resource management in the hierarchy: "we need a waste incineration plant. Waste sorting lines are only suitable for the 'fresh stuff', the waste that has just been collected and is being taken to a sorting station at once. The thing is, if waste spends half a year lying in a landfill while the seasons change, it's no longer suitable for sorting. This is why we need a waste incineration plant to simply get rid of the SDW landfill. But this is not a solution for the newly generated waste" (a representative of the academic sector, Kazan).

Rostec has suggested its own technology. According to it, "it is necessary to build 25–30 waste incineration plants" to eliminate waste in Russia. This establishment is responsible for the development of the industrial scheme of the waste reclamation sector based on the "most advanced" current technology called Hitachi Zosen Inova AG. Upon the termination of the combustion process, metals are extracted from the ashes for further usage, the remaining ashes are sent to a landfill, and biogas is used as a fuel, all of which occurs against the backdrop of low emissions of carbon monoxide and nitric oxide that are purified from dioxins and furans given the strict adherence to the technology (Podobedova & Kalyukov, 2019).

However, the case against WIPs is stronger. This technology is neither scientifically credible nor resource efficient, there is no data on the sufficient utilized capacity of the plants, and such a capacity hasn't been justified: "if we take into consideration the law of some easy money, we are talking about the construction of a waste incineration plant in particular. This technology used to be relevant 20 years ago. Currently, countries that are well-developed in this sector, for example, Germany, are giving up on this technology" (a representative of the academic sector, Moscow).

As a rule, the media depict WIPs differently; some media consider it to be a resource-efficient strategy and reflect the opinions of those in favor of this technology, while other sources criticize the construction of WIPs or are neutral about it. Different platforms rationalize the construction of WIPs or the development of a reclamation industry. According to the media, the main risks that could potentially lead to a "waste collapse" are the tendering procedures for determining regional operators, growing utility charges, and interruptions in the removal of MSW from waste collection areas due to the disorganization of the collection and transportation structures (Rukov, 2018). Some representatives of the scientific community criticize the construction of WIPs. For example, the Russian Academy of Sciences did not support the WIP projects in the Moscow region and Tatarstan.

Challenge 3: Slow growth of the reclamation sector and green businesses. Business can be industrial, linear, or environmentally friendly (zero-waste production). It is important to modernize all of these approaches in order to improve the technological processes and conduct the eco-friendly marketing of products. Overall, 2 billion 53.9 million tons of waste were reused in 2018. However, a positive tendency is observed here. Thus, the rate of the beneficial use of waste increased from 40% in 2006 to 60% in 2016. The Moscow expert from the environmental sector mentioned that "in Russia, fresh raw materials are too cheap, while the raw material market is too monopolized (or, rather, 'oligopolized' as the result of the characteristics of the power system)."

The recycled paper market is the leader of the Russian reclamation sector with 2.9 million tons of secondary raw materials employed. It is followed by recycled glass with 7,000 tons of reused materials (28% of it is extracted from raw materials) (Ulanova & Tulohonova, 2013). Unfortunately, the recovery efficiency of plastic- and rubber-containing waste is significantly the lowest (10%–15%), but hybrid enterprises recycling various fractions and compound electronic waste are currently being developed (for example, Taratrade, Megapolis resource companies) "For businesses, the hardest part is the economic model, since it's hard to cover the expenditures. Companies find the solutions suitable for our mentality" (a business representative). "Our mission is to make the priority of recycling higher than that of landfills" (R. Cherednichenko, Waste Reclamation Association).

Challenge 4: No full-fledged waste sorting infrastructure to provide for the reclamation sector. Tulokhonova and Ulanova's observations of the morphological composition of the MSW over 16 years from 1991 to 2007 led to several conclusions that generally coincide with the global trends: the share of plastic that is hardly recycled in Russia grew from 3.0 to 13.8%; the share of glass increased from 4.2 to 11.4%; the amount of metal waste dropped to be a third as much (Ulanova & Tulohonova, 2013). It suggests there should be new recycling facilities built according to the changing waste fractions generated, but it is not happening. In part, the absence of a waste sorting infrastructure is compensated by active nationwide NPOs that organize separate waste collection in their local districts and raise awareness among the population. The expert describe it as the following: "if we manage to turn this situation to support the processing facilities and to establish the infrastructures for the collection of recyclable materials, we will be able to transition to good recycling rates and lesser environmental pollution. Generating less waste is a much more important issue than finding a new way to dispose of it" (a representative of an NGO, Moscow).

Challenge 5: The social aspect (workplaces, inclusive shadow groups managing waste sorting on an illegal basis) is not taken into consideration in Russia, there are no legal documents supporting the development of this sector, and even experts do not consider this issue to be of importance, prioritizing the development of zero-waste technologies. Contrarily, according to the global agenda, the human resource is considered to be the main asset of society in ensuring zero-waste policies (Medina, 2007). In this vein, the social aspect has several areas of development:

- following the environmental justice principles (equal minimal distribution of environmental risks in the form of pollution) (Murray, 2002);
- creation of workplaces (in an environmentally and socially friendly manner, while ensuring the switch of the industrial sector to greener production practices and a redistribution of workplaces) (Mitsikas & Aravossis, 2017; Schübeler, 1996). In Russia, Professional Standard 16.006 "Waste Management Expert" has been developed and is being implemented. It involves training managers whose goals are to ensure the protection of the environment and population from the negative influence of the industrial and domestic waste and to improve the sanitary condition and appearance of cities and populated places;
- looking for informal and exclusive work groups while ensuring the proper level of labor protection (garbage workers, immigrants, the poor). The representative from NGO describes it as the following: "shadow economy can be dangerous when there is a lack of workplaces while the labor of garbage workers is being automated, it leads to social tension";
- making the production system more eco-friendly and providing advanced training of workers in the area of eco-friendly standards.

The Ministry of Industry and Trade of the Russian Federation and the Ministry of Natural Resources and the Environment plan to supplement the existing central and federal system with a new element represented by public-private partnership and launch a new MSW management system, where the government might cover up to 30% of the expenses for the establishment of the reclamation industry (Minprirody planiruet sozdat', 2018). The most common topics covered in the media are investments into the reclamation sector, the problems of tariff formation and increasing product prices that depend on the size of environmental charges, and legal characteristics of granting licenses in the waste and waste reclamation sectors (according to the polluter-pays principle). The main investors are Gazprom, Rostech, ST – Invest, RosNano, and Hitachi Zosen Inova. The Rosatom State Corporation is supposed to build seven large complexes for the reclamation of industrial waste of hazard classes I and II by 2024 (Rosatom do 2024 g, 2018).

Prospects of the sector development were assessed by experts who outlined several possible scenarios:

- *The pessimistic scenario*: The state of the waste management system grows worse than 5 or 10 years ago since there is no "typical scenario for the development of separate waste collection and reclamation." Given the increasing rate of waste generation, "the amount of waste grows, but it's not being recycled"; the resources required for the restoration of the ecosystem are depleting. Business representative describes it as the following: "currently, waste-related issues are stemming from the fact that the population is motivated, people have collected signatures and conducted surveys proving that the population is ready, while the authorities aren't. It's not enough to install separate waste collection containers to solve the issue, it's necessary to establish an infrastructure."
- *The stagnation scenario*: According to this scenario, "nothing is changing," "the amount of recycled waste is not changing," and "there will be no separate waste collection for at least 20 years more" (representatives from academic and professional communities).
- *The positive (constructive) scenario*: Experts describe this scenario with caution (no great progress is observed, but there are supporting blocks created that will help to build the institute of zero-waste economy in the future). This point of view features several positions:
    - *The path of local changes* associated with specific solutions of individual issues, such as amending the legislation, ameliorating the territory,

boosting public involvement, expanding the share of separate waste collection, and installing garbage containers for waste sorting. Individually, none of these changes can grant a solution to the major issue, but they provide the infrastructural support required to solve it. The positive scenario implies implementing effective local measures at specific enterprises: "at most large enterprises, technologies that allow to reduce the negative impact on the environment are being implemented... As a result, we observe lower emissions to the atmosphere and environmental monitoring" (an NGO representative, Moscow).

- *The path of changes that can be characterized as a shift in waste-disposal technologies, but not in the area of resource-efficient policies.* There are changes in the legal, economic, and technological infrastructures, but they are developing according to "the law of easy money rather than common sense, especially when it comes to the construction of waste incineration plants. This technology used to be relevant 20 years ago. Currently, countries that are well-developed in this sector, for example, Germany, are giving up on this technology" (representative of the academic sector, Kazan).

The expert society supports the idea of a circular economy but suggests adapting its elements to fit the typical challenges observed in Russia. The element of centralization in the waste management system that is being reformed should be preserved when it comes to ensuring national and international standards of zero-waste production and consumption, but there should also be local amendments introduced to the federal law developed in the regions of Russia (Fig. 5.1). In Russia, the concept of a zero-waste city implies the balance of elements and the development of such components as eco-friendly technologies (eco-parks, sorting stations, waste reclamation industry, smart emission, and waste monitoring technologies), eco-management (eco-friendly laws and a regional operator that monitors the whole life cycle of commodities), economy (higher environmental taxes and benefits, ensuring "green" workplaces in the area of waste management), and culture (development of eco-friendly habits, stronger NPOs, environmental equality).

When it comes to the state leverage on businesses in the area of waste management, there are three means, such as fines, fees for negative influence, licensing, taxes, and utility fees outside of the scope of the legislative policy. Government representative from Moscow describes it as the following: "The first two support measures are investors' equity holding and the provision of guarantees for loans, borrowings and other investors' obligations. We still need to finalize the provision of guarantees to banks for investors, the provision of interest rate compensations, cofinancing, and the compensations of

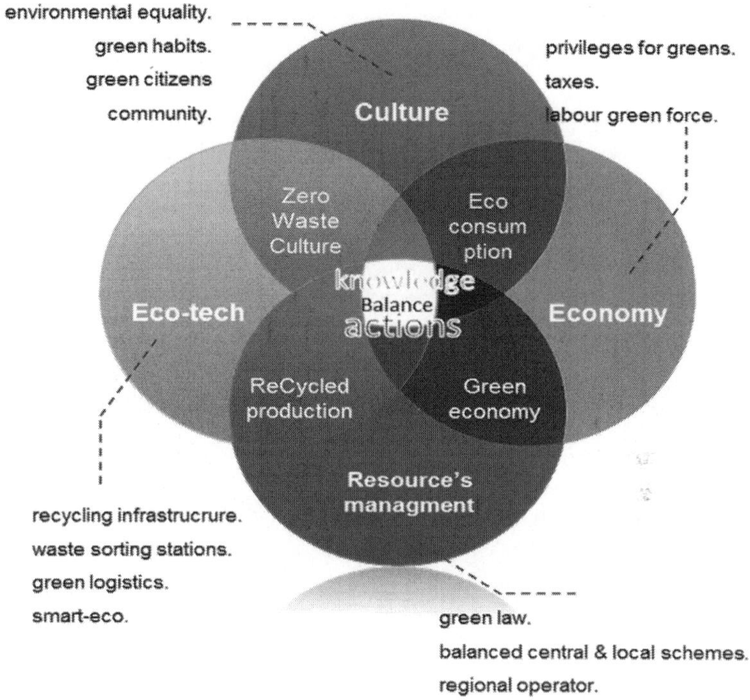

Fig. 5.1. Experts' Scheme of Zero-waste Management in Russia.

capital investments". It is important to establish an eco-friendly closed cycle of waste management in Russia and design a financial model that will comply with the reform when it comes to the full set of measures associated with the complete life cycle of commodities, from production to reclamation.

RUSSIANS' WASTE MANAGEMENT PRACTICES

On January 1, 2018, the Federal government decreed separate waste collection. According to the Ministry of Natural Resources, the new complex MSW management system is aimed at introducing fundamental changes to the principles and mechanisms of waste collection, sorting, reclamation, and disposal, as well as at the amelioration of environmental well-being. "I think the reform is going rather well. The majority of the territorial subjects of the Russian Federation have switched to the new MSW management system. That is, 69 territorial subjects. Some of them have already implemented the new system in full" – Dmitry Kobylkin, Minister of Natural Resources (Musornaya reforma, 2019).

However, public polls conducted in Russia showed the opposite: by 2019, the dynamics had not changed, and only 7% of the Russian population sorted their waste, which was the same in 2012 (Ministry of Natural Resources and Environment of the Russian Federation, 2017b). A study conducted by the researchers from the Higher School of Economics (Shabanova, 2019) showed that the group of people intending to get involved in waste sorting (potential participants) (19%) along with those intending to continue participating in separate waste collection and sorting amounted to 29%. The majority of Russians (68%) have never participated in this practice and are not going to start sorting waste in the upcoming couple of years (indifferent). Compared to 2014, the number of people participating in waste sorting hardly changed, which signifies that this practice will not develop if the current conditions are preserved, in the scientists' opinion (Shabanova, 2019).

The authors' poll of the citizens of Moscow and Kazan showed that approximately 23% of them regularly (always, often, or from time to time) practice waste sorting (plastic, glass, paper) at home, while 36% of the respondents had never done it. These data are somewhat different from the nationwide average. It is safe to suggest that the efforts associated with the introduction of a separate waste collection infrastructure have been more prominent in such advanced Russian cities as Moscow and Kazan than in all of Russia on average.

We employed the heuristic advantages of the contextual theory suggested by Paul Stern (Stern, 2000) in order to determine the reasons for the population's (non)involvement in separate waste collection practices.

Thus, we asked the population to name the major obstacles preventing them from practicing separate waste collection. The main reasons for the nonrecycling group include the lack of necessary infrastructure to serve domestic residences (68%) and the lack of will (21%) and time (21%), while 12% of residents do not know how to do it. The representative from environmental NGO describe it as the following: "People who understand that waste is a problem and are trying to recycle are very few; most of them think that waste is not their problem and they switch the responsibility from themselves to the governmental officials". The lack of will was commented by experts in the following manner: "A bulk waste container has been installed nearby. It's also great, it's wonderful. However, it also shows the level of culture of our people. Many of those who live nearby are too lazy to go to the usual containers now, so they throw their usual garbage bags into the bulk waste container because it's closer to their home" (a representative of the academic sector, Kazan). Thus, the convenience factor noted in foreign research devoted to the establishment of separate waste collection practices in developed and developing countries is one of the key factors in Russia (Kirakozian, 2016; Miafodzyeva & Brandt, 2013).

Public polls and expert interviews reveal a strong opinion that to adapt to separate waste collection practices, the population must know for a fact that it will be more than just for show. During the interviews, some experts doubted that the rubbish from the containers was genuinely going to recycling and utilization for many reasons ("not economically efficient," "low quality of recycled raw materials," "poor development of the recycling industry," etc.). However, some of the experts mentioned that "although the recycling might be a performance act – 'pokazyha' – this can become the first steps in 'normalization' of the recycling in Russia and for its residents" (representative from the academic community).

Certain economic factors can act as external and internal advantages of switching to separate waste collection, such as receiving additional income from giving sorted waste to special separate waste collection stations, composting food waste for further use as a fertilizer within the household, adhering to sustainable consumption due to ethical and economic reasons, etc (Shabanova, 2019). Ethics and the desire to minimize waste and switch to eco-friendly consumption (Ilyin, 2000; Trentmann, 2007) are some of the factors forming the positive identity of an environmentally responsible consumer. Hence, according to the authors' poll, 7.8% of the citizens of Moscow and Kazan compost their food waste, 16.5% of them recycle hazardous waste (batteries, lamps, etc.), 10% of them provide textiles for recycling or reclamation, and sort waste at home into different fractions (plastic, glass, paper) are 8.5% (Fig. 5.2) On the figure presented practises that always using citizens in their daily life only.

According to the nationwide poll (Shabanova, 2019), when it comes to separate waste collection practices, selfish motives are not prevailing (only 11%

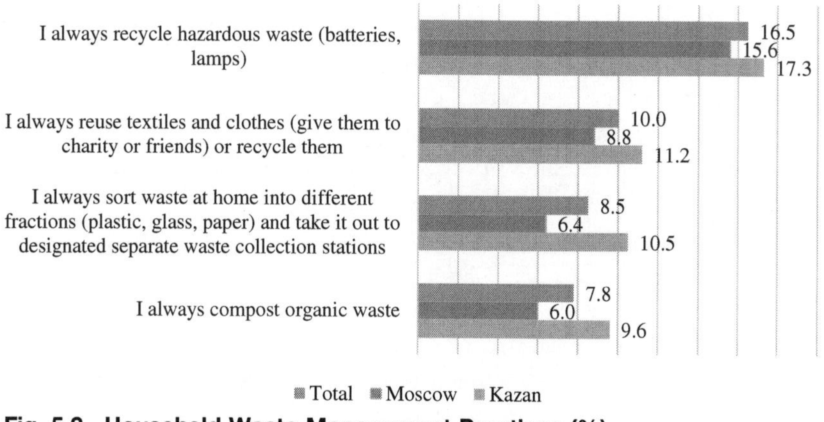

Fig. 5.2. Household Waste Management Practices (%).

of the respondents named one or more personal benefits), not exclusive (even among those few who named personal reasons, more than a half supplemented them with altruistic superindividual considerations), or differentiating when it comes to getting involved in separate waste collection practices (the differences between different groups on these grounds are statistically irrelevant, ranging from 11 to 14%).

ENVIRONMENTAL INEQUALITY, WASTE-RELATED CONFLICTS, AND PUBLIC ENGAGEMENT

Among all Russian regions, Moscow Oblast remains the most loaded with municipal waste, where the forced shutdown of landfills has already resulted in a new conflict related to waste and an increase in the protest activity among the citizens (Ermolaeva, 2015; 2019a). The capital of Russia generates 1/5 of all domestic waste in the country (11 million tons). 10% of this waste is being incinerated at four WIPs, while the rest is being disposed of at landfills whose resources have already been depleted. The problem of environmental security is especially pressing for the territories neighboring cities. Thus, while comfortable urban space is being created in Moscow, environmental conflicts are rising in less economically developed municipal districts neighboring the capital.

The scale of protest activity in the Moscow region was bigger than any other social or political protest actions. Massive open-air landfills and the pollution they bring are stirring tensions across Russia, provoking some of the most sustained protests. Thousands of people have defied police bans to march against planned landfill openings, blaming the mounting piles of garbage for health problems and foul-smelling air. Locals complain that the often overpowering stench from the garbage causes headaches, nausea, and other health issues, while eco-activists have reported dangerously high levels of nitric oxide and hydrogen sulfide in the air (Bennetts, 2019).

According to the Presidential Council for Human Rights of the Russian Federation, at the beginning of 2019, protests associated with waste-related issues took place in 30 regions of Russia (Obolensky, 2019). The most critical hotspots of tension appeared almost simultaneously in different communities of Moscow Oblast, such as Volokolamsk (Yadrovo landfill), Odintsovo, Malinki, Voskresensk, Kolomna, Krasnoarmeysk, Serpukhov, Balashikha, Klin, and Dmitrov, where protests were registered. The authorities of Tver Oblast refused to accept the waste coming from Moscow since it was considered to be an issue of the "environmental safety of the region"; the same happened in Kolomna in December 2018.

One of the most high-profile conflicts between local citizens and the government is unfolding in association with the Yadrovo open-air landfill. Protests against the construction of the landfill began in March. The conflict escalated when several children got poisoned because of the hydrogen sulfide emissions coming from the landfill at the end of March 2018. Mass protests demanding that the landfill be shut down began near Volokolamsk Central District Hospital on March 21. To solve the problem, local authorities underwent personnel replacements and took a number of emergency measures regarding the landfill. However, the protest activity did not cease to exist, and activists formed action groups to monitor the landfill and organized spontaneous rallies. On April 1, 2018, approximately 5,000 locals took part in a protest on the central square of Volokolamsk, demanding that the governor of the Moscow region be dismissed and the landfill be closed. Locals were also protesting by filing legal claims against the Yadrovo open-air landfill (Steshenko, 2018). Extensive coverage of the public hearings in the media and the dissatisfaction with the environmental policy and the political regime played a great part in the advancement of civic interests. Citizens living in the vicinity of the intended waste disposal facilities actively promote combined forms of activism, such as picketing approved by the authorities, demonstrations, hunger strikes, and various active means of digital activism (petitions, pollution-tracking mobile platforms).

The media is extensively covering hunger strikes, civic unrest, and protests. Such media as Izvestia and RIA Novosti pay attention to the lack of public hearings and the systematic inequality between the periphery and the capital, as well as between different regions. For example, when it comes to waste logistics between the regions, the authorities of Tver Oblast refused to accept the waste coming from Moscow since it was considered to be an issue of the "environmental safety of the region"; the same happened in Kolomna in December 2018, as well as in Arkhangelsk and Murmansk, thanks to environmental activists. This proves the complexity and necessity of developing local life cycle assessment schemes, refining inner logistics, and working on the matters of economic and ethical responsibility of waste owners in Russia.

The media coverage of such topics is typically accompanied by references to ministries and municipalities, seldom NPOs, activist communities (Narodniy Front, Green patrol, Greenpeace), or waste collection and transportation companies (Khartia). At the beginning of 2017, the media often covered the Clean Country program, whereas now the Ecology project is more popular (Chistaya Rossiya, 2019).

Waste-related conflicts became one of the most populous protest actions in Russia over the past decade and a new milestone in the development of civic activism in the country. Despite the well-documented fear, cynicism and fatigue of Russian people participating in the protest activities, and general paternalistic values, these cases illustrate that for the first time in far too long, Russians have begun to regain their sense of "right to the city," solidarity, and public dialoge. Through well-coordinated collective actions, building alliances and coalitions with different stakeholder groups, employing multiple strategies that tackle various public arenas including mass media, NGOs Russian raised public awareness and made the case visible politics. This also moved the disengagement discourse into the legislative level and forced governmental authorities to enhance people's ownership of public policies.

The chapter demonstrated that the Russian system has a waste management scheme at the state, regional, and municipal levels. Each region is provided with a regional operator that collects, transports, distributes among enterprises recycling, and, for the final destination, waste disposal at landfills and incinerators. Challenges for the Russian waste management system include only a few recycling enterprises, an increase in the number of garbage plants and the number of landfills, and unpopularity among Russians for the practice of separate waste collection in households, which provoke social conflicts and environmental inequality. The achievements include the controlled centers with regional operators with digital databases that increase the efficiency of communication, benefits and subsidies of green enterprises, and a growing influence of the NGO sector. The main reasons for the non-recycling group include the lack of necessary infrastructure to serve domestic residences and the lack of will and time.

6

PUZZLE 5: GREEN AND BLUE ZONES

O. Basheva and I. Kuznetsova

Living in a city restricts people's access to nature and makes them more exposed to such negative environmental factors as noise and air pollution. According to experts from the World Health Organization (WHO), the optimal use of green zones and other nature-related solutions is an innovative approach that improves the quality of life in cities, increases the resilience of local communities, helps to develop a sustainable lifestyle, and enhances citizens' health and well-being. The creation and maintenance of parks, playgrounds, and green spaces in public areas help to provide citizens with sensible opportunities to be in touch with nature while preserving and supporting biodiversity in an urban environment, and reducing such environmental hazards as air, water, and noise pollution. Public green zones mitigate the consequences of extreme weather conditions (heat waves, extreme rainfalls, floods, etc.), improve the quality of life in a city, and improve the health and well-being of citizens (see Hartig, Mitchell, de Vries, & Frumkin, 2014). WHO believes that green zones should be easily accessible to all the groups of the population and equitably distributed inside cities (World Health Organization Regional Office for Europe, 2017).

WHO distinguishes a wide range of measures in the area of urban greening, such as developing green spaces along roads, streets, and railways, setting up small urban green zones (for example, gardens or micro parks) and green playgrounds; implementing green roofs and facades; providing parks and urban lawns; designing waterside routes or trails that connect green and blue (water) zones; and providing easier access to city parks, urban forestlands, and natural wildlife zones.

There is evidence that having access to parks and performing physical activities in green zones has a direct impact on life expectancy and prevents numerous diseases (see e.g., Wolch, Byrne, & Newell, 2014). In social geography, there has been much discussion about the concept of therapeutic landscapes (see Williams, 1998, 2017) that dwells on the range of effects an environment has on the physical and mental health of a person. The development of urban green spaces can be paradoxical and does not necessarily achieve environmental justice as it can also increase housing costs (Wolch et al., 2014), and as studies conducted in Moscow demonstrated, the city's flagship parks became the key arena of neoliberalization and commercialization (Büdenbender & Zupan, 2017; Zupan & Büdenbender, 2019).

This chapter addresses the current state of the green and blue zones in Moscow and Kazan, and the contradictions within the municipal policies that invest money in parks when preparing for mega-events and in the course of urban beatification, on the one hand, and neglect the ecological condition of green and blues zones, on the other hand. The accessibility of green and blues zones for the population has been analyzed, and there has been professional assessment of current urban policies and the role of ecological activism.

THE CONDITION AND MAJOR PROBLEMS OF GREEN AND BLUE ZONES IN RUSSIAN CITIES

In Russia, urban greening and beautification principles are listed in the concept of comprehensive beautification of public spaces (Koncepciya kompleksnogo, 2018). The document includes requirements for the reconstruction and flexible provision of planting of trees, bushes, and flowers in streets and parks, installation of fences, architectural lighting of streets and districts, hardscaping and installation of urban design objects. In practice, the green zones of large Russian cities are significantly reduced because of the construction and renovation of motorways, expansion of urban settlements, and the active development of high-rise communities in place of former agricultural lands and villages. The major issues of urban greening in large Russian cities are associated with the lack of a systematic approach to greening and an insufficient involvement of private enterprises in urban greening since this niche is monopolized to 80%–85% by state and municipal enterprises which restrict the access to greening for small businesses (Panchuk, 2015). The price of land occupied by buildings and infrastructure elements is significantly higher than the price of land occupied by green spaces. Consequently, the commercial structures involved in urban development are tempted to opt for more financially beneficial construction works.

Different evaluations of Moscow's green zones and their condition are offered in sources provided by the official establishments and non-commercial environmental organizations. In 2014, Greenpeace used satellite images made by Landsat and geographic information systems to estimate that only one third of the city is covered in vegetation (Zelenyye nasazhdeniya, 2015). In 2015, a survey conducted by the same organization showed that Muscovites believed that Moscow had become less green over the past few years.

The city has lost 636 ha of woody vegetation since 2000, mostly in the west and in Zelenograd, while the Southwestern District remained relatively untouched. According to Greenpeace, the decrease in the number of trees and shrubs is also accompanied by the reduction of green spaces necessary for the provision of health and safety regulations. On average, there is 31 sq m of land covered with trees and bushes per resident in Moscow, which complies with the current city planning regulations. However, these figures do not reflect the actual situation, since this indicator varies significantly depending on the district: the figures vary widely from 3.1 and 3.8 sq m in Novokosino and Maryino districts to 827 sq m in Molzhaninovsky district with a population of 3.8 thousand people and 314 ha of forestlands. In 63 districts out of 125, there is less than 25 sq m of green land per resident. Occasionally, lands belonging to nature reserves are excluded from environmental protection and used for urban development causing a "loss of valuable environmental properties" (Kolesnikov, 2015).

Other sources provide a more positive picture. According to comparative research provided by PwC, Moscow was one of the greenest cities in the world (compared to New York, Singapore, Hong Kong, Beijing, Shanghai, Seoul, Berlin, London, Sao Paulo, Tokyo, and Mexico City) in 2009–2016 (Klyuchevye vyvody, 2017) with more than half of its territory occupied by green spaces. According to Moscow's official open data portal, there are 780 park amenities in the city (OPEN DATA Moscow City Government, n.d.), while other official sources provide a much smaller number of 436. Nevertheless, in 2010, there were only 130 park amenities and 86 recreational zones. Over a period of five years, visitor attendance at parks in the summertime increased almost fourfold. There are reports stating that more than half of the territory of Moscow is covered with vegetation, while the share of park amenities comprises 12.2% (Moscow Mayor Official web-site, 2013).

The general city plan of Kazan indicated that in 2019, there were 49 sq m of green spaces per resident in the city (Semerkin, 2019). At the same time, green spaces only occupy about 98 sq km of the city, which comprises some 23% of its total area and falls behind the regulations.

Both cities experienced the common tendency of many post-socialist cities to pursue regrowth, new construction and development on the one hand, and the preservation and enhancement of green spaces on the other (Haase, Dushkova, Haase, & Kronenberg, 2019). The government played a crucial role in these strategies which has been characterized earlier by Kinossian as urban entrepreneurialism and state-led metropolization (2012, 2017).

Over the past few years, extensive beautification works have been undertaken in many Russian cities, and cities are at the cutting edge of these changes. Beautification and greening programs are encapsulated in different strategic documents. In 2013, the Moscow City Government launched the Million Trees campaign to add vegetation to the yards of residential buildings. In 2015, the campaign was also implemented in the territories of social establishments. Since 2015, a large-scale beautification program called "My Street" ("*Moya Ulitsa*") has been carried out. Aside from the development of existing parks, new ones were established, for example, Zaryadye Park near Kremlin, whose role in urban greening and huge cost were perceived with skepticism by a number of experts; the park remains, however, a brand image project of the development of downtown Moscow.

Since 2015, the President of the Republic of Tatarstan has personally monitored the intensive development of park amenities in Kazan. As a result, the existing parks were beautified and several new parks were created. Some experts note than new green recreational areas were developed on the territory of existing forest zones or green areas, whereas it is necessary to increase the number of green zones by developing wastelands and urban spaces lacking trees. There are many micro districts in Kazan with no green recreational zones whatsoever. The dense development of the city center is not accompanied by the creation of additional green spaces; on the contrary, trees are being cut down, which has a negative impact on the air condition combined with the increasing traffic load. The master plan for Kazan, which is currently being discussed, features a new section called "Nature and Recreation Complex" that will list existing green zones, formalize their legal status, and establish threshold indicators of green areas for each new micro district.

In 2018, almost all media coverage of urban greening was associated with these programs, especially in the media of Kazan, while in the national media, Izvestia and RIA Novosti often referred to them. These media sources have separate sections devoted to beautification (#Greening, #My_Street, #Beautification, #Parks, #Ecology, and #Renovation). All of them list the achievements of the city management and everything is framed in a positive light. The major topics are the plantation of new trees and shrubs, flower beds and flower gardens, the beautification and reconstruction of parks and stadiums, and the beautification of residential yards and recreational zones, etc (V Moskve na blagoustroyennykh, 2017; V parke 850-letiya, 2018).

Overall, the media of Moscow presents the beautification project in a positive light. RBK is the only media group to publish several critical notes associated with the high cost and long duration of the program (Sardzhveladze, 2018), as well as the losses incurred by the catering businesses located on the streets that were included in the program (Demidova & Novopashina, 2017). RBK also highlighted the poor engineering preparation for the program (for instance, now, whenever it rains, large puddles form on Myasnitskaya Street), and the importance of having a more sensible approach to work and coordinating it with the citizens (not all Muscovites like the way the urban beautification is conducted, some consider it excessively expensive).

The Kazan greening and beautification agenda is mostly covered by the local media and regional branches of the federal media (RBK Tatarstan). In this case, news items with different subject matter were covered, such as the installation of free Wi-Fi outside apartment buildings (Sychev, 2017), expenses involved with the beautification of parks and water bodies (Sotnik, 2017), the city master plan (Tat'yana Prokof'yeva, 2017), and fines for parking in green zones (Rylova, 2018).

In the autumn of 2017, a municipal program called "Development of a comfortable urban environment in 2018–2022" was mentioned several times at a public commission hearing (V Kazani proekt formirovaniya, 2017). The preliminary list of public spaces drawn on the basis of citizens' requests (as well as with the help of the "Map of Destroyed Roads" project) included 32 sites, while the list of courtyard territories included 2,065 sites. The package of beautification works in public areas included the installation of walkways, lighting, sprinkler systems, CCTV, wireless Internet, mass cultural event sites, sports grounds, dog parks, portable toilets, fountains, as well as greening and hardscaping. As for the courtyards, asphalt repairs, extension of pass ways, construction of lay-bys and pavements, installation of lighting, hardscaping, and greening are planned. The media also covered the new master plan of Kazan proposing the renovation of the city center (Tat'yana Prokof'yeva, 2017).

It is hard to find statistics on the breakdown of green zones in city districts in the media. The experts interviewed during our research study believe green zones are unevenly distributed:

> *The cityscape varies a lot in Moscow. The best practices of street narrowing, installation of bike lanes and pedestrian zones, beautification of public zones, greening, etc. are being implemented in the city*

> *center. However, everything changes outside the Garden Ring Road, where every piece of land is being used for construction, even if there is vegetation on it.*
>
> *(a representative of an environmental NGO, Moscow)*

Even though every district has a park or a public garden, this might not be sufficient provision:

> *There are large natural spaces in the city, which is amazing, but it would be deceitful to say that the city is immersed in greenery, given that some districts only have one small park exclusively accessible by the residents living next to it.*
>
> *(a representative of NPO, Kazan)*

Moreover, while it is possible to arrange the green zones in an environmentally friendly way in new districts, it is impossible to change the situation radically for the best in old districts.

Some of the experts believe that the green framework of the city is being destroyed as the green spaces are being reduced because of construction works. Many trees, even in Special Protected Natural Areas, are being cut down, the condition of green zones is deteriorating, and the authorities are prioritizing their economic interests rather than the development of territories. Current greening regulations are being disregarded, while manipulative strategies are being employed, for example, when annexing the so-called New Moscow, some forestland was also annexed to the city, thanks to which the official statistics showed positive results as the green areas of the city had been augmented.

As for the relevance of such green zones for the population, a mass survey showed that 47.7% of Muscovites and 45.7% of Kazan citizens sometimes walk in parks and public gardens, and 35.3% of Muscovites and 27.6% of Kazan citizens do so regularly (Fig. 6.1). Urban blue zones are almost as essential: 47.9% of Muscovites and 40% of Kazan citizens sometimes go out to rivers, channels, ponds, and lakes located in the city, and 16.1% of Muscovites and 14.1% of Kazan citizens do so regularly.

Almost all experts consulted during our survey note that technically, municipal authorities started paying more attention to green zones, and the green areas of the cities of Moscow and Kazan are large overall compared to other cities: "*We have many parks. Indeed, the area of green zones is rather vast in our city compared to other cities of the same scale*" (a representative of the academic community, Moscow). The development of green zones is being well-subsidized. At the same time, some believe that there are not enough

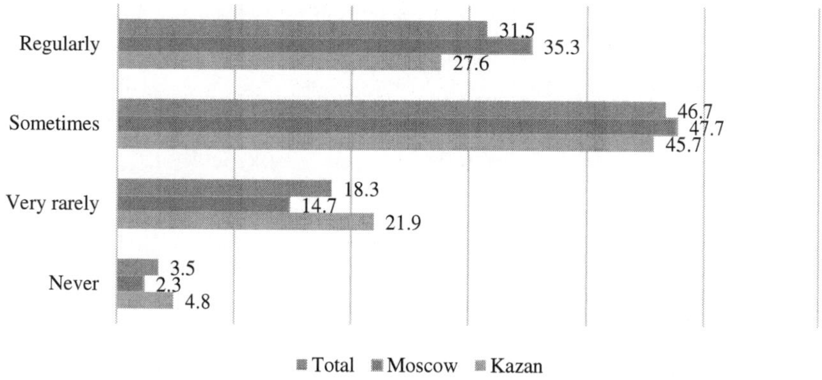

Fig. 6.1. Do You Walk in Parks/Squares and Outdoor Recreation Areas in Your City? (%).

green areas, and the measures aimed at their preservation are insufficient, since the financial interests of real estate developers are given precedence over protecting the ecology:

> *In my opinion, there are no measures taken for the preservation of flora and fauna. The quality of water might be alright, but the animal life is being disregarded .... Whenever it is possible to build an apartment building and a parking lot in a green zone, it is done. The green zone isn't preserved. Whenever it is possible to sell a green zone to businessmen who would cut down the trees and build some sort of an eco-park there, it is done for the sake of business, and it is money that is prioritized, not the common sense.*
>
> *(head of environmental NPO, Kazan)*

Usually green zones are accessible by transportation, but this is mostly true for large parks. Parks are not always accessible by bike lanes. The experts believe that there are not enough green zones accessible by foot in Moscow,

> *Since they are few now, they became accessible for the population by transport, but overall... this is a critical issue. ... Ideally, every resident should be able to leave their house and easily find a green zone nearby. Whether it's a green courtyard, a park, or a flower garden. Green spaces should be situated within walking distance from houses.*
>
> *(head of an environmental NPO, Kazan)*

In part, these observations were proved by a mass survey. Over one third of the population noted (37.2% of Muscovites and 36.4% of Kazan citizens) that it takes no longer than 15 minutes to reach the closest park or flower garden from their houses. For 29% of the population (29.9% of Kazan citizens and 29.5% of Muscovites), it takes 15–30 minutes to reach a park. It was found 14.7% of Kazan citizens and 12.7% of Muscovites have to use public or private transport for 15–30 minutes to reach a park, while 12.3% of Muscovites and 9.7% of Kazan citizens arrive at one in less than 15 minutes by transport. Only 7.2% of Muscovites and 6.7% of Kazan citizens need more than half an hour of transportation to reach the closest park.

Experts interviewed complained about the quality of maintenance of urban green zones and have questions associated with the responsibility for such maintenance, since it is not always attributed to the competent institutions:

> *Unfortunately, the number of conservation officers is being reduced in our forest zones, or their work is being restricted, and they are prevented from tree pruning, which is their duty. There are hardly any conservation officers in Bitsevski Park. For some reason, it's state-financed entities who take care of the trees.*
>
> *(a business representative, Moscow)*

> *Motorways... Consequently, no one is trying to save flora or fauna, because it's much easier to cover the snow with reagents in winter and cover the soil with lawns in summer. Such lawns die, but they just bring more soil, plant seeds, they turn into grass, the grass is mowed, and for some time, everything is green and pretty again. Nobody cares about the environment here.*
>
> *(head of an environmental NPO, Kazan)*

The description of conflicts associated with the reduction of parks, cutting down of trees, infill constructions, etc., does not appear often in the media, but sometimes it happens. In an expert's opinion, "*...people fight for their green zones, but sadly, real estate developers usually win*" (head of an environmental NGO, Kazan). A mass survey showed that the conflicts between citizens and authorities (5% in total) or businesses (2% in total) usually happen because of the reduction of green and blue zones, despite the decrease being rather small-scale. In Moscow, citizens most often came into conflict with the local authorities because of the construction of motorways, highways, buildings, gas stations, parking lots, etc. in green and blue zones (40% of the citizens surveyed reported participating in these conflicts) and because of the felling of trees (35%). In Kazan, one third of the participants in such conflicts entered them because of the construction of a waste incineration plant (32.4%), slightly less than 30% participated in them because of the construction works conducted in green and blue zones, and 20.6% protested against the felling of trees.

For example, the residents of the Novo-Savinovskiy district of Kazan and eco-activists fought against the real estate development of the right bank of the Kazanka river and the destruction of a park, but lost to the authorities. Importantly, that park was all that was left of a large natural area on the right bank of the Kazanka river that had been systematically destroyed over the past few years. First, it was used for the construction of facilities designated for the Universiade-2013, then for a parking lot for the FIFA World Cup (Grigorieva, 2019; Kazan Activists, 2016).

Experts interviewed also noted several cases of fighting for green zones associated with opposition to the construction of churches in green spaces: "The *Russian Orthodox Church is always threatening to build standardized churches in all available places. My activist friends sometimes have to protect parks from it*" (a female representative of an environmental consulting agency).

The citizens of Kazan and Moscow actively fought proposed development by businesses because of the real estate development in green and blue zones (53.3% of Muscovites and 50% of Kazan citizens answered that they participated in conflicts against businesses). The citizens of Kazan fought against the felling of trees more often than Muscovites (28.6% against 13.3%), as well as against garbage dumps and the pollution of territories (21.4% against 13.3%).

Nevertheless, a number of experts noted positive changes associated with the programs mentioned earlier. Moscow City Government allocates considerable funds for urban greening, and the city of Moscow provides some of the highest funding when it comes to investing in environmental protection according to an expert involved in community councils under the ministries administrating the city.

Experts list a number of issues associated with the infrastructure of parks situated outside of the city center, such as droughts, lack of spring planting, bare zones, falling trees and trees in critical conditions, and the presence of litter. The environmental condition of parks and flower gardens is poorly monitored, since there is no systematic approach to environmental monitoring in Moscow according to experts (most of who work for private enterprises or NGOs); at the same time, other experts refer to the activity of Mosprirody in this area.

As for the public opinion, according to the results gathered during our research survey the citizens of Moscow and Kazan consider the condition of parks to be average, at 3.8 out of 5 (excellent state). Citizens mostly appreciate the cleanness, the well-tended appearance (3.9 in Moscow, 4 in Kazan) and the proximity of parks (3.9 in Moscow, 3.8 in Kazan). The presence and condition of playgrounds is slightly less appreciated (3.7 in Moscow, 3.9 in Kazan), as well as safety (3.7 in Moscow, 3.8 in Kazan). When it comes to the availability of cafes, restaurants, and coffee houses, the citizens of Kazan rated their parks higher than Muscovites (3.5 in Kazan against 3.2 in Moscow). At the same time, the dynamics show that citizens positively appreciate the changes associated with urban green zones. More than half of citizens (57.1%) think that the number of green zones increased over the past five years. However, more Muscovites than Kazan residents think that the situation did not change (31.8% against 25.2%), and more residents in Kazan than Moscow who believe that the situation deteriorated (15.6% in Kazan against 9.1% in Moscow).

Aside from green zones, blue zones are also very important for cities. Moscow and Kazan feature numerous water bodies. There are over 200 watercourses in Moscow, including the eight rivers (Moscow, Yauza, Setun, Gorodnya, Skhodnya, Nischenka, Desna, and Pakhra), and over 600 water bodies (Moscow Department for Environmental Management and Protection, n.d.).

Almost half of all Muscovites (47.9%) and 40% of Kazan citizens state that sometimes they spend time next to rivers, channels, ponds, and lakes in their cities; 16.1% of Muscovites and 14.1% of Kazan citizens do so regularly, while 36.8% of Kazan citizens and 28.8% of Muscovites seldom spend time in such activities. The quality and well-tended appearance of water bodies received the score of 3.3 (3.28 in Moscow and 3.25 in Kazan), and 42.7% of Muscovites and Kazan citizens believe that the condition of the blue zones has not changed over the past five years (the citizens of Kazan are more prone to thinking this way at 44.3% against 41.2% among the Muscovites). It was reported that 35.2% of citizens see some improvements (38.1% of Muscovites and 32.4% of Kazan citizens), and 17.4% believe that the condition of blue zones deteriorated (19.1% of Kazan citizens and 15.8% of Muscovites think this way).

Expert opinions and monitoring results show that the environmental condition of water bodies is poor in both cities. In Moscow, the authorities have barely addressed the issue of cleaning water bodies over the past 20 years. The main sources of pollution of Moscow rivers are the unauthorized run-off from urban territories and the coastal wash-offs (Kramer & Tikhonova, 2015; Stecenko, 2016). Experts evaluate the condition of water bodies in Moscow as poor because many of them are situated next to hazardous and harmful industrial enterprises that dump their waste into the water. Moreover, real estate development also adversely affects a number of water bodies because many developers simply dump their waste into rivers. There is an issue of unauthorized filling up of water bodies for the sake of real estate development, several cases of which occurred in the Old and New Moscow. However, the biggest problem is the lack of planning for the preservation of the green framework of the city and, consequently, blue zones.

Volunteers and professional divers play a big part in cleaning the blue zones of Moscow, even though the local authorities have also started to clean up water bodies.

When evaluating the condition of water bodies in Moscow, one of the environmentalists expressed an opinion that there is a contradiction between the environmental requirements for water bodies and the mindset of citizens who perceive urban water bodies as recreational sites:

> *It's a twofold problem. From the environmental point of view, water bodies must remain untouched, there should be fish, birds, dogs, otters swimming and bathing in them. We used to have otters in our pond here, in Ochakovo. From the citizens' point of view, a pond should be a place for them to swim in, and the city administration has to find a way to balance things here .... They want to know that they can just go to a pond and have a swim there without catching anything, without worrying that something terrible might happen to them.*
>
> *(head of an environmental NPO, Moscow)*

The main blue zones of Kazan are lake Kaban, Kazanka river, and Kuybyshev reservoir (Volga river), all of which are in a poor condition. Both official sources (Ministry of Ecology and Natural Resources of the Republic of Tatarstan, 2019) and expert surveys show that these water bodies are rated as "dirty" according to their hydrochemical composition. The main pollutants are organic substances, ammonia nitrogen, and oil products (see Kondratieva, Vibornova, & Ismailova, 2013). The number of water bodies available for swimming within the city limits is decreasing annually. The development of the banks of rivers and lakes also negatively affects the condition of water resources. The banks of the Kazanka river are being built on for the sake of real estate development because it flows in the city center, where economically and touristically attractive sites are situated (Nabiullina, 2019). As a result, unique species of flora and fauna are disappearing. Access to water and walkways along water bodies is being limited to official embankments, whereas just a few years ago, there were numerous routes available for walking and jogging. Local environmental activists protested against the real estate development and the filling up of Volga river and several small water bodies in the Zaimischa district, Kazan, but it did not change the situation (Grigorieva, 2019).

There are several lakes in the suburbs of Kazan which are in a rather poor condition. However, there are a few positive changes, such as the ecological restoration of Lake Lebyazhye near Kazan (see Oktyabrev, 2018).

The chapter shows that there are discrepancies in the data related to the share of green zones in cities, as some sources provide higher values, while others artificially augment the statistics through manipulative strategies involving annexing new territories or reorganizing existing forestlands for parks (which obstructs the evaluation of the dynamic changes in green areas). On the other hand, the uneven distribution of green and blue zones is also explained by a number of objective reasons, for example, it is almost impossible to perform an eco-friendly renovation of older districts. As for the population, the majority (57%) notice positive changes associated with urban greening that have happened over the past five years. Green zones are in demand (for example, in Moscow, the visitor attendance at parks in the summertime increased almost fourfold over the period of five years), but for about 30% of the population, the parks are still inaccessible by foot. Blue zones are also considered to be popular recreational sites among the population, as almost half of Muscovites (47.9%) and 40% of Kazan citizens say that sometimes they spend time near water bodies, such as rivers, channels, ponds, and lakes in their cities. However, the citizens only give the score of 3.3 out of 5 for the quality and appearance of such water bodies, and 42.7% of the citizens of Moscow and Kazan do not think that the condition of water bodies has changed over the past five years. An expert survey also showed that, for example, in Moscow, the issue of cleaning water bodies has been barely addressed over the past 20 years.

7

PUZZLE 6: ENVIRONMENTAL GOVERNANCE AND POLITICS

O. Basheva, V. Korunova, and I. Kuznetsova

"Good governance" has been at the center of local sustainability discourse after the adoption of the UN 1992 Rio Declaration on Environment and Development which states that "good governance" is a precondition for achieving sustainability at the local level (Evans, Joas, Sundback, & Theobald, 2006). As de Cruz, Rode, and McQuarrie mentioned,

> *The Urban Governance Survey shows that cities have developed an incredible array of institutional mixes to both manage challenges and deal with their national governments, but multiscalar relationships are decisive.*
>
> *(2019, p. 10)*

What are the main patterns of urban governance in regard to sustainability in Russian cities, and to which degree are the public and ecological experts involved? How do the population and eco-activists raise the agenda of ecologically safe cities and what are the obstacles to widening the participation in urban governance? These are the issues explored in this chapter.

ECOLOGICAL POLICY IN RUSSIAN CITIES: DEINSTITUALIZATION, LACK OF STRATEGY AND BARRIERS TO PUBLIC ENGAGEMENT

The environmental policy of Russian authorities has been established over many years and has reflected changes in economic interests and political powers. Russian environmental policy is also characterized by a high degree of wildlife preservation and a heavy load on the human environment. Even though the collapse of the Soviet industry in the 1990s reduced the impact of industry on the city environment, its effects are still very high in large cities (Lyakhovenko & Chulkov, 2017). The environmental policy of Russian cities is characterized by a number of structural and legal problems as well as implementation issues.

The ruling documents of Russian legislation and the strategic development plan of the country and its territories stipulate the goals and objectives of Russian environmental policy, though they are not viewed as of primary importance. According to the Russian Constitution, natural resources are described as pivotal in the life of the Russian people, but the use of natural resources should harm neither the environment nor people. The strategic documents of Russia proclaim the country's natural resources and the issues associated with them as among many factors that allow it to be a world leader in economic and social development. For example, the Concept of Long-term Social and Economic Development of the Russian Federation until 2020 (Koncepciya dolgosrochnogo, 2018) considers the government policy which places less importance on issues of freshwater scarcity and climate change in Russia give the country a competitive advantage.

This policy also determines the choice of strategic lines of development for the cities in question, Moscow and Kazan. The Project of Moscow Socio-economic Development Strategy until 2025 refers to the ecology of the city as the balance of relationships between the many living conditions there. The low ecological quality of living conditions within Moscow makes it impossible to actualize the competitive advantages of Moscow as a global development center. The Socio-economic Development Strategy of the Municipal Entity of the City of Kazan until 2030 also defines ecology as the condition of the urban environment among many other factors. Its high quality, in turn, ensures the stable economic growth of Kazan and its transformation into a global city. However, the trend of environmental development is hardly perceptible in the strategic documents of Moscow and Kazan.

The amalgamation of the environmental organizations and structures responsible for the exploitation of natural resources in the 1990s impacted on the structural and legal aspects of environmental policy. It reduced the role of environmental policy in strategical decision-making and implementation of environmental monitoring. The absence of a clearly outlined urban strategy at the federal level in Russia and the neoliberal logic of urban development (Golubchikov, Badyina, & Makhrova, 2014), the erosion of environmental protection institutions and weak law enforcement throughout the post-Soviet period (Newell & Henry, 2017) are significant factors in the growing environmental issues in Russian cities. Commenting on the lack of ecological concern in the state agenda during the 1990s, Yanitsky called that period "de-ecologization" (2018c). Mol described the situation with environmental governance in Russia as deinstitualization stating that "from the early 1990s onwards, the federal institutional structure for environmental protection has been systematically dismantled and undermined, without significant new environmental institutions" (2009). Therefore, the position of environmental institutions in urban governance is very vulnerable (Khaliy & Levchenko, 2017). As Golubchikov (2017, pp. 272–273) mentioned,

> *...there is still much room to reveal how post-socialist urban space has been an intensive and oft-cruel battleground ...to reveal different agencies in these rapid and complex processes – state, markets, and people – in their different embodiment, organization, and personification.*

The capacity of civil society to take part in environmental policy is influenced by the reduced role of the organizations for nature preservation mentioned above and the lack of functional democratic institutes of public engagement in the area of city management (see, for example, Henry, 2010; Evans, 2012). The "Foreign agents" law was followed by the reduction of funds of NGOs and led to the closure of some of the organizations together with decreasing engagement by the population (Javeline & Lindemann-Komarova, 2019; Tysiachniouk, Tulaeva, & Henry, 2018). Also, from 2010 Russia has banned unapproved protests with more than one person. All these factors significantly limit the ability of civil society to participate in urban governance, especially in regard to urgent environmental conflicts which require public action. The major urban transformations and ecological initiatives are led by the cities' authorities and do not provide many opportunities for public engagement.

RECENT PROGRAMS OF ENVIRONMENTAL GOVERNANCE IN MOSCOW AND KAZAN VIA THE PRISM OF PROFESSIONALS' OPINIONS

Recently, both cities adopted several strategic programs for urban development and ecological governance. In Moscow, such projects were the "Green Technopark" and "Smart City," strategic projects "Smart City–2030" and

"New Environmental Policy of Moscow until 2030"; in Kazan, there were "Kazan – the Territory of Health," "Kazan – Diverse Agglomeration Center," "SMART City Kazan," and "The Strategy of the Environmental Safety and Development of the Natural and Resource Complex of the Republic of Tatarstan for 2017–2021 and Prospects for 2030." The various programs indicate that in Moscow several policy measures are being taken in the area of air cleaning (the introduction of public buses featuring an engine compliant with an emission standard equal to or above Euro 5), urban greening ("Million Trees" project), urban beautification ("My Street" project), etc. In Kazan, there are measures aimed at air cleaning (the introduction of public buses featuring an engine compliant with an emission standard equal to or above Euro 5), water bodies cleaning ("The Year of Water Conservation Zones – 2–16"), and urban greening ("The Green Record," "Blooming Kazan," "The City of Parks and Flower Gardens – 2015").

As the framing of the environmental issues are regulated by and depend on the dominant governmental interests (Ermolaeva, Ermolaeva, Kuznetsova, Basheva, & Korunova, 2020), most of the mass media materials in regard to ecology in Moscow and Kazan were focused on authority-led initiatives and less on ecological conflicts.

Despite the evident similarities between the legislative frameworks for conducting environmental policies in cities and the similar media coverage, the efficacy of measures implemented in Moscow and Kazan vary greatly according to official reports. For instance, Moscow and Kazan are 2nd and 18th, respectively, in the Rating of the Environmental Management of Russian Cities 2015 (the rating is drawn by the Ministry of Environment and Natural Resources of Russia; there were 55 cities assessed in total) (Rejting ekologicheskogo upravleniya, 2015). According to the environmental rating of Russian cities in 2017, the situation is reversed, with Moscow being the 16th, and Kazan being the 2nd (the rating is designed by experts of the All-Russia People's Front in association with the Ministry of Natural Resources of Russia; there were 103 Russian cities evaluated overall) (Ekologicheskij rejting, 2017). At the same time, the experts included in the survey assessed the efficacy of the environmental policies conducted by the local authorities in both cities as poor (at 2.4 out of 5).

In both cities, experts believe that there are positive changes in the environmental policy, but they are rather superficial while the core problems remain unresolved or even worsen.

The experts interviewed feel some of the greatest achievements of the environmental policy in Moscow are the implementation of beautification and greening programs: "Much money is spent on greening… Moscow is trying to implement some measures and conduct a reasonable environmental policy according to its budget and capacities" (a representative of the academic society, Moscow). Progress is seen in the inclusion of corporate sustainability into the official agenda of local authorities

> *There are events where local authorities speak about it, and each announcement of the kind is a significant development for us... yes, it's mostly just words for now, but earlier, there was nothing at all. So, if I were to speak less critically, some things are still changing for the best.*
>
> *(a female business representative, Moscow)*

The development of green constructions, green transportation, and corresponding infrastructure are also believed to be important:

> *The number of bike lanes is insignificant, but they exist. There are about 50 charging stations for electric vehicles... The carsharing program is developing nicely, it worked well for the city. Pedestrian zones appear....*
>
> *(a male NPO representative, Moscow)*

In Kazan, according to the experts interviewed, the local authorities' achievements in their environmental policy are limited to decisions associated with urban greening and beautification: "They started paying more attention to parks" (a female representative of the activist sector, Kazan),

> *Development of green zones. Naturally, it's something positive. Five years ago, it was hard to imagine having parks. It always seemed, if there's no food to eat, why would anyone care for parks? It always seemed to be unattainable. Everything has a good side.*
>
> *(a female representative of the activist sector, Kazan)*

> *The trend of urban beautification, there have been several changes over the past few years; they are quite noticeable. The beautification of the city center, of the key sites, key points, parks, flower gardens that are being developed.*
>
> *(a professional male environmentalist, Kazan)*

However, the experts believe the inner heterogeneity of Moscow creates issues and impediments preventing the implementation of successful environmental policies in the city. The obsolete infrastructure and networks complicate the establishment of green practices and technologies: "Evidently, the infrastructure is in a horrible state, it has been since the Soviet era. It's only getting worse every year" (a male representative of the academic society, Moscow).

It has been noted that urban greening and beautification projects are often implemented for publicity purposes and do not envision any structural changes. For instance, an NPO representative noted that

> *The cityscape varies a lot in Moscow. The best practices of street narrowing, installation of bike lanes and pedestrian zones, beautification of public zones, greening, etc. are being implemented in the city center. However, everything is different outside the Garden Ring Road... No measures are taken there for the establishment of bike lanes, pedestrian zones, or charging stations for electric vehicles, etc.*
>
> *(a male Muscovite)*

Several experts also consider the initiatives in the area of park development implemented in Kazan to be undertaken for the sake of publicity,

> *I think it exists for the sake of PR promotion. Yes, they do plant something, but take basic compensatory planting, for example... When they cut down all perennial trees and plant spruces along the highways, knowing that they will all perish in two years... This is wrong. It sounds good, it seems to be done to make it all pretty, but the results are null.*
>
> *(a female representative of the activist sector, Kazan)*

As a result, image-building initiatives are given priority over the issues associated with waste management:

> *Something is being done, it is clear that they are trying to beautify the territory, but it is dubious, as always, because, on the one hand, the authorities establish the Zaryadye park and such, while there are enterprises like ZIL that, as is known, dump their waste into the sewage uncontrollably.*
>
> *(a female business representative, Moscow)*

The lack of penalties for environmental offenses remains a major problem.

Weak and selective law enforcement for violations of the ecological laws is yet another issue. As one of the NPO activists mentioned, "A large share of procedural irregularities goes unpunished by the authorities, which creates the atmosphere of absolute permissiveness. Nobody bears liabilities of the violation of environmental regulations" (a male NPO representative, Moscow).

According to the majority of the experts surveyed, in both cities, the main issues are inconsistent decision-making, poor coordination between different departments and institutions, and the lack of multiscalar relationships between different stakeholders and communities.

As one of the government representatives noted,

> *There is almost no coordination between different departments of the city... The right hand doesn't know what the left hand is doing, and nobody knows where the head is. This is why the environmental policy of the city is in a very poor condition.*
>
> *(a male representative, Moscow)*

This echoes the opinion of an ecological activist,

> *Coordination... I don't think it exists. In my opinion, coordination means more than just passing one request from one department to another. Each one of them has to try and do something from where they stand....*
>
> *(a female activist, Kazan)*

One of the scholars remarked that this issue does not only exist at the city level, it is also present at the federal level, "There is no adequate communication between the government agencies at the federal level" (a male representative of the academic society). Some professionals stated that despite the documents on urban development including the structure of relations and communications for decisions in environmental governance, in the reality, the ecological policy is very weak. As one of the environmentalists mentioned, "Overall, I consider the environmental policy of the city authorities to be, first and foremost, incomprehensible. I have seen no defined environmental policy of the kind" (a male environmentalist, Kazan). An academician echoes this opinion,

> *Everyone works on their own. Despite the fact that the provisions of the Ministry of Natural Resources and Environment stipulate the coordination of all departments, including the ones of the territorial subjects, I don't see that happening.*
>
> *(a male representative of the scientific society, Kazan)*

Based on this, some experts even talk about the absence of an environmental policy as such, "The most important part is that we don't have a policy" (a professional male environmentalist, Kazan).

Many experts noted during their interviews that environmentalists are usually involved in governmental work to comply with official procedures, but their evaluations are often disregarded:

> *Potentially, they have no influence. There is a public council under the Department of Environmental Management... As far as I can see, the work of this public council is reduced to writing scientific research projects, but it does not go further than that.*
>
> *(a male NPO representative, Moscow)*

It has been noted that collaboration on the part of the authorities is not productive but only to provide the illusion of meaningful participation,

> *No, their voices have no weight in the decision-making process, they simply have a position and are invited to all those meetings for... just so that they can write in the report that there was an environmentalist present at the meeting. But they have no weight, nothing....*
>
> *(a female representative of the activist sector, Kazan)*

Moreover, environmentalists are often involved in work after decisions have already been made,

> *The decisions are being primarily made based on the economic interests, then social matters are being taken into consideration, while the environment is often simply used as a cover-up for these decisions. Environmentalists are set to justify the wise decisions of the authorities... As a rule, they are unable to affect such managerial decisions because the environmental aspects are only discussed after the decision has already been made.*
>
> *(a professional male environmentalist, Kazan)*

Some activists also note that professional environmentalists from Kazan are unwilling to influence the resolution of environmental issues in the city, "They simply don't pose such questions, see? For them. it's easier to make the calculations and say how much something would cost. There's no fight there whatsoever..." (a female representative of the activist sector, Kazan). This echoes the opinions expressed in an interview with one of the professional environmentalists who considered her role to be instrumental:

> *Being an environmental engineer, I can say that all construction projects receive an environmental assessment. There is research,*

> *when it comes to constructions, the impact for the period of construction and exploitation is being evaluated*
>
> *(a female environmentalist, Moscow)*

She indicated that she usually does not provide the ecological evaluation during the later stages of project implementation.

Thus, the neoliberal interests of urban development are often prioritized over the environmental needs, and the lack of inclusivity and public and expert engagement in environmental governance impedes sustainability in Moscow and Kazan.

CIVIC ENGAGEMENT IN ENVIRONMENTAL GOVERNANCE

The low possibility of public engagement in the resolution of environmental issues is one of the central problems of the environmental policies in both cities. The experts included in the survey estimated the capacity of the population to affect decisions impacting the urban environment as poor, at 2.2 and 2.3 out of 5 in Moscow and Kazan, respectively. This is the result of the unwillingness of the authorities to cooperate with the population and to consider the issues of the people. For example, according to a business representative from Moscow, "The authorities hardly listen to the population when it comes to this… There is no collaboration between the public and the authorities."

The same is true for the procedure of public hearings that is supposed to ensure consideration of the public opinion, but essentially is a mere formality in the experts' opinions: "Public hearings are of recommendatory nature. It is sad, but true… The recommendatory nature is not very effective" (a professional female environmentalist, Moscow). A similar opinion was voiced in regard to the public hearings in Kazan, "They are ineffective because those participating in the public hearings hardly listen to each other. So, despite formally holding a public hearing, decisions that would satisfy everyone are not found" (a male representative of the academic society, Kazan); "As of now, no big-scale project goes without public hearings… They organize the meetings, people propose something… But it's hard to say it's effective" (a professional male environmentalist, Kazan). Public hearings are seldom covered by the media.

According to many respondents, the authorities often act in a "closed" manner; they are not ready to resolve the environmental issues of the city together with the public,

The problem lies in the mentality of the officials who are used to making decisions behind the scenes and believe that they know better. When it comes to decision-making, it's much easier and more comfortable for them if no one gets in their way....

(a professional male environmentalist, Kazan)

However, the exception is the planning of public spaces and parks in Kazan and a number of initiatives in Moscow involving the representatives of different public groups.

The survey results reveal the population and also estimates their possibility of participating in the resolution of environmental issues as low (Fig. 7.1).

The situation has hardly changed over time. Half of the surveyed citizens of Moscow and Kazan (50.8% and 53.3%, respectively) think that their ability to affect the actions of local authorities and enterprises on environment issues did not change over the past five years. Similar shares of the respondents (60% in Moscow, 56.1% in Kazan) also believe that the local authorities poorly engage the public in the resolution of environmental issues. In the public opinion, the attention local authorities pay to the environmental issues in cities has not changed either (49.8% in Moscow, 50.1% in Kazan), and it is currently assessed as mild (3.09 out of 5 in Moscow, 3.11 in Kazan). The degree of transparency and availability of information on different environmental indicators for the parties concerned has hardly changed (54.4% in Moscow, 50.4% in Kazan). The surveyed citizens of Moscow and Kazan assess it as medium (3.2 and 3.02 out of 5, respectively), while experts deem it to be below medium (2.5 for Moscow, 2.6 for Kazan).

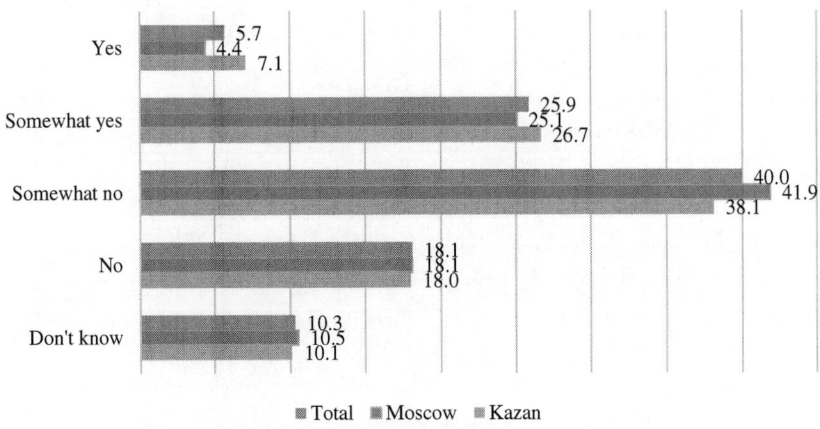

Fig. 7.1. In Your Opinion, Are Local Authorities Actively Involving the Population in Environmental Decision-making? (%).

In line with the data provided above, the majority of citizens of Moscow and Kazan have never written letters about the environmental problems they are concerned with to the relevant authorities and have never participated in public hearings and discussions devoted to environmental issues. Only 9.2% of Muscovites and 8% of Kazan citizens wrote such letters, and only 10.8% of Muscovites and 8.8% of Kazan citizens participated in public hearings and discussions. At the same time, the poor level of public engagement in the resolution of environmental issues is not defined exclusively by the "closed" nature of the authorities. Several experts suggested that the population is insufficiently concerned with environmental problems. In part, it is explained by the difficult social and economic conditions, "Most people are preoccupied with surviving… the environment is not visible" (a professional male environmentalist, Kazan). There is also an opinion that the population is more involved in environmental policies when it concerns their residential areas, "The public engagement in the environmental and municipal policies is limited to the citizens' attempts to preserve the environment outside their windows" (a male representative of the authorities, Moscow). At the same time, examples were given of how the population seemed untroubled despite the fact that certain decisions were directly affecting the environmental condition of their districts. For example, according to a business representative from Moscow,

> *Here's a good example, in my district of Lefortovo, we were defending a flower garden near Sputnik cinema when the authorities wanted to dig a construction pit there for a new subway station. First of all, we found little support from the locals; it was very difficult to engage them, to deliver a message that it's important to them, that they need the garden for walks. It's one thing when you come to an event with activists, motivated people, businesspeople, entrepreneurs working on this issue, and it's a different story when it's just the population as it is.*

Echoing that, an ecological activist from Kazan noted, "I was deeply shocked when I realized that the residents of Bugulminsky District are unconcerned with this issue, even though their children are getting sick according to the data."

According to the Muscovites included in the survey, the top five most urgent environmental conflicts for the city are infill constructions (55.6%), the cutting down of trees (46.5%), unauthorized dumping sites (43.5%), the construction of malls in residential districts, and the construction of waste incineration plants (24.9% each). As for Kazan, the top five most urgent environmental conflicts for Kazan are the construction of a waste incineration plant (51.9%), unauthorized dumping sites (48%), the cutting down of trees

(41.7%), the filling up of water bodies (37.1%), and infill constructions (32.8%). Fig. 7.2 below provides further details.

Overall, 3.5% of the surveyed citizens of Moscow and Kazan participated in environmental conflicts against the authorities and businesses. As the survey showed, in Moscow, such conflicts usually concerned infill constructions and the construction of new buildings in green and blue zones, while in Kazan, they were mostly associated with the cutting down of trees and the construction of a waste incineration plant (further information is available in the chapters devoted to waste management). In roughly half the instances, the population did not succeed in achieving the desired outcome (44.4% in Moscow, 40.4% in Kazan).

At the same time, in the experts' opinion, civic engagement in all of its forms (raising awareness among the population, writing letters to the relevant authorities and services, protest action) is the most efficient way of influencing the environmental policy of local authorities. As one of the scholars interviewed noted, this is a right granted by the Constitution which is often being

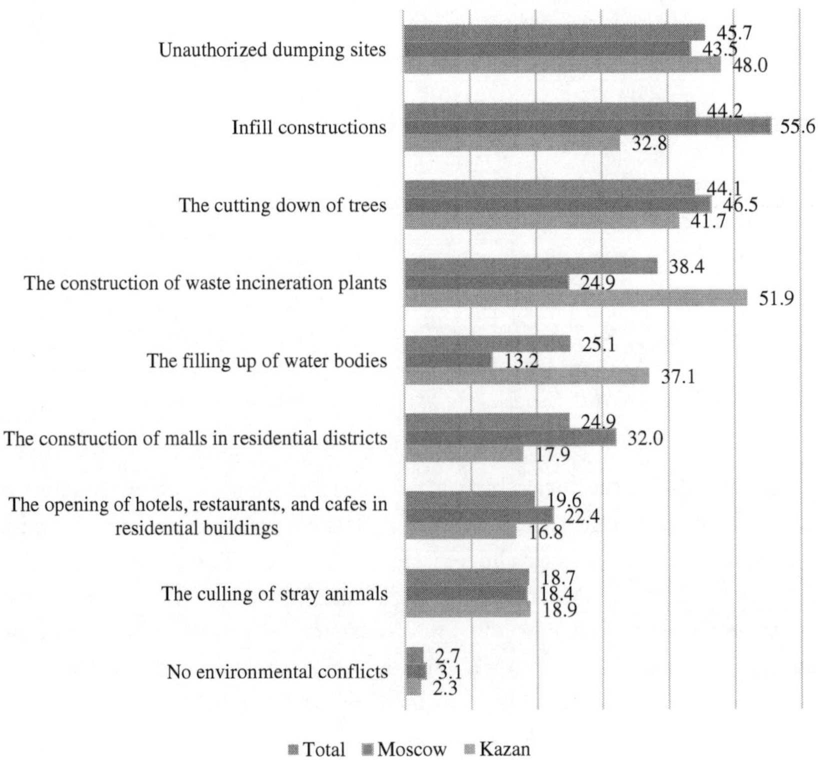

Fig. 7.2. The Most Urgent Environmental Conflicts Stated by the Population (%).

disregarded by the authorities, "Let's start with the Constitution, it says, every citizen has the right for a healthy environment. Citizens must demand being provided with a healthy and high-quality environment" (a male academic, Kazan). One of the environmental activists interviewed said that such an engagement must include all available legitimate methods,

> *The methods of combat should include not stopping at what has been achieved, it's when you use everything you can to stop a construction project or... on the contrary, when they are trying to destroy something, you don't just write a letter to one government agency, you go to a protest, you involve other people, you raise awareness among your neighbors and acquaintances, you start writing to all the authorities, you call them....*
>
> *(a female environmental activist, Kazan)*

The lack of attention on the part of the local authorities to the environmental concerns of the population restrains bottom-up initiatives. As one of the business representatives mentioned in an interview, it is crucial to develop communication between the government and the population, "because if people try to give their opinion and are ignored, they stop trying."

The chapter highlights that despite the fact that environmental issues are part of the strategic development plans in both cities, in reality, a number of problems arise, such as the ambiguous nature of environmental legislative provisions, lack of interdepartmental interaction of authorized bodies when making and implementing managerial decisions, and an almost complete exclusion of professional environmentalists and public representatives from this process, or their involvement as a pure formality. Even though only a small portion of the citizens of Kazan and Moscow in the survey show their concern for environmental issues to some degree, the public effort in combating waste incineration plants and protecting the green zones should not be overlooked. However, the civil ecological activism did achieve the desired results in the majority of the environmental conflicts.

CONCLUSION

P. Ermolaeva, Y. Ermolaeva, O. Basheva, I. Kuznetsova, and V. Korunova

Nowadays, there are many social and economic methods to assess how sustainable the city is, for example, the Index of Sustainable Development of Cities in the Russian Federation (SGM, 2015) and the Environmental Performance Index (Korotkov, Trubyanov, Zagainova, & Nikonorov, 2015) among others. They perform diagnosis of the development of cities on their way to sustainability improvement. The scientific challenge lies in the fact that, despite availability of studies on the assessment of greening processes in Russia's cities (Korotkov et al., 2015; Medvedeva, Kozenko, & Komarova, 2015), there are no comprehensive studies on the assessment of the behavioral, technological, and economic "readiness" of different groups of Russian citizens for transition to "sustainable" city standards, new environmental values, behaviors, and technologies. The book aims to overcome the gap and provide the results of the only study in Russia, which focuses on a comprehensive study of the social-environmental situation and sustainability issues in Russian cities from the perspectives of various stakeholders.

In our study, we define "sustainable city" as a city combining high efficiency and innovativeness; a city where the population is provided with the best possible living conditions; a city that persists through constant change. We consider a city to be a socio-biotechnical system, that is, an open system of non-linear connections and interactions, in which technical, environmental, economic, and social aspects act as integral characteristics of a whole. The changes of urban systems are complex, dynamic, systematic (the changes occur in several systems at the same time), and the trajectories of changes originate from the interactions between multiple systems, which cannot be reviewed within the scope of mono-disciplinary approaches. As such we analyzed various socio-environmental indicators of urban sustainability via theories of environmental inequality, socio-psychological theories of the environmental behavior, the zero-waste approach, and the principles of a circular economy.

The analysis showed that in Russia, the principles of sustainable urban development are found in numerous strategic documents, federal and regional laws, and its territories. Collectively they seek to deliver the key component of Goal 11, "Make cities and human settlements inclusive, safe, resilient, and sustainable," of the United Nations Agenda 2030 for Sustainable Development. However, there is no systematic or consistent implementation of the principles of the sustainable development of Russian territories, enshrined in laws and regulations. At the governmental level, sustainability is perceived as a means of satisfying the need of the government and society for the economic well-being and development of the environment and in the realization of smart sustainable city goals in the digitalization of the urban environment.

In the book, an in-depth analysis of key components of socio-environmental sustainability of Russian cities such as air and water quality, sustainable transport and mobility, energy efficiency and energy consumption, waste management, green and blue zones, environmental governance and politics from the positions of various urban stakeholders are introduced. Based on the data, we suggest strategies on how to promote sustainable cities in Russia.

AIR AND WATER QUALITY

Official statistics on the air quality in Russian cities are not always available, and their accuracy is disputed by independent environmental organizations. The unavailability of sensible statistics on air pollution signifies that this indicator is insufficiently included in the city planning process. Air pollution is directly linked to social inequality since it has a negative impact on the health of the population who do not have the financial opportunity to move to an eco-friendlier area. It is apparent that air pollution will remain a pressing issue and will continue to cause conflicts between the population, businesses, and authorities related to the atmospheric pollution coming from landfills and waste incineration plants. The lowering of pollution standards related to several components of atmospheric air quality, the unwillingness of the authorities and businesses to invest in a more advanced and less toxic waste recycling system, as well as the crackdown on environmental activists, signifies the likely development of a negative air pollution scenario. Transport will also have a negative effect on air quality if trends remain the same. Namely, if traffic continues to increase, infill constructions continue to develop, the traffic load on city streets increases, and the population is not stimulated to transition to eco-friendlier means of transportation, the negative effect of exhaust gas on the atmosphere will continue to increase.

The quality of the water supply, including the safety of tap water, has been consistently improving in Russia and especially in big Russian cities over the past few years according to the official data. According to this research study, the quality of the water supply in Moscow is rated higher by the surveyed experts and local population than in Kazan. In the experts' opinion, the pre-emptive policy implemented by the authorities in Moscow over the past five years ensured a significant improvement of the processes of water withdrawal, purification, and transportation and ameliorated its quality. However, the results achieved are only perceived in part by the population who are generally satisfied with the water supply quality but do not notice the positive trends. Policies conducted by the authorities of Kazan are met with more criticism by the experts as the policies do not contribute to the improvement of the quality of the water supply in the city. In the experts' opinion, the numbers of the related problems with the water supply are not changing or growing, which is also mirrored in the opinions of the local population. The citizens of Kazan are less satisfied with the quality of tap water in their city than Muscovites and employ domestic means of water purification or purchase bottled water more often than the citizens of Moscow.

Policy Recommendations

To improve air and water quality in cities, the following actions are necessary: (1) to include the issue of air pollution in the process of city and spatial planning and to conduct modeling of the air quality while taking into consideration different factors associated with transportation, waste, and production; (2) to improve the geographic accessibility of eco-friendly public transport and to increase the number of free parking lots near subway stations; (3) to take measures to increase the demand for electric and hybrid vehicles; (4) to ban the placement of landfills and waste incineration plants near inhabited areas and to provide compensation for people moving from districts near landfills; (5) to provide public and accurate data on air pollution in cities for the population; (6) improving the quality of the water supply in both cities requires prompt action from local authorities; (7) in Moscow, the monitoring of industrial enterprises should be strengthened; (8) Moscow industry should be provided with central sewage collection systems; (9) sanctions for dumping pollutants into water bodies should be toughened; and (10) in Kazan, it is important that the local authorities change their attitude to water supply problems and prioritize improving the quality of water in the city.

SUSTAINABLE TRANSPORT AND MOBILITY

The initiatives of city authorities in the field of sustainable transport and mobility development include the development of public transport, car sharing, bicycle routes, and light rail systems. However, there are a number of unresolved problems that are exacerbated by the constant increase in the number of personal vehicles. These include the use by city residents mainly of personal vehicles, the imperfections of the public transport system, the serious environmental burden because of the use of vehicles with gasoline and diesel engines, the low level of development of alternative modes of transport, and the inconvenience and insecurity of bike and foot routes. The main strategies for improving the environmental friendliness of the movement are switching public transport to gas fuel and developing personal and public electric transport. However, many experts doubt the environmental friendliness of gas fuel because during gas combustion steam is released, which contributes to the strengthening of the greenhouse effect. According to experts, hydrogen engines and electric vehicles can provide an adequate solution. However, for the latter to operate, new capacities are needed for the production of electricity, and therefore there is an urgent need for the development of alternative energy sources. And if the development of public electric transport is assessed very positively by experts, the proliferation of electric cars causes some skepticism (because of climatic conditions, long distances, and the lack of infrastructure in Russia).

Policy Recommendations

Sustainable transport and mobility in Russia can be promoted by the development of public transport (increase in the number, frequency and speed of movement of public transport, increasing the number of routes, increasing passenger comfort); improving the organization of traffic (restriction of entry and a partial ban on parking in the city center for cars, construction of intercepting, and paid parking in the city center); development of bicycle infrastructure; creation of pedestrian zones; and, the application of tariff policies that stimulate the use of public transport by citizens.

ENERGY EFFICIENCY AND ENERGY CONSUMPTION

There are two priorities in the energy program of Russian cities: (1) energy conservation and energy efficiency of the hydrocarbon complex and (2) the gradual increase of the energy obtained from renewable sources. In cities, the digitalization and changing priorities of the transport energy system are advancing rapidly, while renewables are being developed slowly because of the powerful lobby of traditional energy sources. Experts believe there is no significant difference between Moscow and Kazan with the prospects of energy saving and energy efficiency; there are energy systems using economical and eco-friendly equipment, smart technologies, housing and utility communication systems, a search for possible applications of RES in different economic sectors and constructions, replacement of traditional sources of energy, revision of the energy and industrial life cycle at enterprises, reduction of the number of inefficient heat pipelines, eco-friendly types of fuel for public and private transport, and zero-waste production. A survey showed that citizens are well aware of the connection between energy-efficiency, energy conservation, and cost-saving, and the latter stimulates them; 60–65% of the population is involved into different resource-saving practices. The centralization and monopolism of the energy structure bears the advantages of continuity and reliability of the power supply utilities, but also raises barriers to developing a decentralized renewable energy system that tries to exist within the same unitary system.

Policy Recommendations

To achieve the SDGs in sustainable energy, Russia has to (1) quickly scale up the potential of renewable sources of energy and prepare the economic foundation in the form of economic tools for both state and private companies; (2) negate the economic and environmental risks for the traditional and renewable energy sectors. Such risks are represented by the monopoly of enterprises in traditional hydrocarbon energy sources, disbursements of the economic model based on the export of raw materials, and external global economic conditions forming the dependency of the GDP on selling hydrocarbon fuels. There are also latent and unplanned risks, such as the mutual relations and interests of local operators and the natural threats impeding the development of RES; (3) pay more attention to the real opportunities of the internal and external implementation of the renewable sources of energy. As for Russia's external energy geopolitics, there is a potential for using and implementing RES in Asian countries (Kazakhstan, Mongolia, and China), Baltic countries, Scandinavia (Finland), and CIS (Belarus). Internal prospects are manifested in the possibility of using future profits to develop other infrastructures, including the social infrastructure of the regions where the application of RES is the most relevant; and (4) although the use of most renewable energy sources in cities is unavailable or restricted, it is possible to consider using low-grade heat sources and isolated RES stations as emergency energy.

WASTE MANAGEMENT

The Russian system has a waste management scheme at the state, regional, and municipal levels. Each region is provided with a regional operator that collects, transports, distributes among enterprises recycling, and, for the final destination, waste disposal at landfills and incinerators. Challenges for the Russian waste management system include only a few recycling enterprises, an increase in the number of garbage plants and the number of landfills, and unpopularity among Russians for the practice of separate waste collection in households, which provoke social conflicts and environmental inequality. The achievements include the controlled centers with regional operators with digital databases that increase the efficiency of communication, benefits and subsidies of green enterprises, and a growing influence of the NGO sector. The main reasons for the non-recycling group include the lack of necessary infrastructure to serve domestic residences, the lack of will and time.

Policy Recommendations

When developing a scheme for adapting the concept of a zero-waste city in Russia, it is important to introduce the following systematic instruments: (1) the eco-friendly technologies suitable for the industrial profile of an individual city (eco-parks, sorting stations, waste reclamation industry, smart emission, and waste monitoring technologies); (2) enhancing the legal aspect at the nationwide level (upping the sanctions against the negative impact on the environment and increasing the pollutant's accountability, expanding the legal role of an operator that controls all phases of the life cycle assessment in waste producing and recycling); (3) implementing economic incentives (higher environmental taxes and benefits, creating "green" workplaces in waste management); and (4) creating social tools that can establish an environmental culture (developing eco-friendly habits and practices among the population with the help of different social institutes and agents). The successful promotion and adaptation of separate waste collection practices requires the combined effort of different groups of stakeholders, such as the population, the government, businesses, NPOs, and the media. In cooperation with businesses, NPOs, and the media, the government must take measures to develop the supporting infrastructure represented by a dense network of stations for separate waste collection, easy-to-use and convenient separate waste collection containers, a system of incentives for environmentally responsible citizens and a system of sanctions for non-compliant citizens, a mass media campaign, etc. As for businesses and private operators in particular, they have to ensure timely removal of waste from the territory adjacent to houses. As for the population, citizens must be ready to invest their time and other resources into separate waste collection practices while being supported by economic, legal, and ethical factors.

GREEN AND BLUE ZONES

Over the past 10 years, many strategic documents clearly defining the development goals for urban green zones were drawn up for Moscow and Kazan. In addition, several beautification and greening programs were launched, which makes the policy aimed at the preservation and development of green and blue zones more viable than before. The majority of media sources, especially the local media, mostly focus on the achievements of municipal services in the area of beautification and greening programs, hardly ever covering problematic topics. Experts consider the efforts in urban greening to be some of the most successful and noticeable elements of environmental policies, while noting that these efforts tend to be mostly declarative than actually feasible since several problems are associated with prioritizing economic interests over environmental ones, delegating the responsibility for green zones to institutions disinterested in this matter, and the unequal distribution of green zones among districts. Blue zones are considered to be even more problematic because of the unauthorized filling up of water bodies for the sake of real estate development and dumping of industrial waste into rivers. However, the biggest problem is the lack of a reasoned strategy for the preservation of the green framework of the city and, consequently, blue zones.

A desk study and an expert survey show that there are discrepancies in the data related to the share of green zones in cities, as some sources provide higher values, while others artificially augment the statistics through manipulative strategies involving annexing new territories or reorganizing existing forestlands for parks (which obstructs the evaluation of the dynamic changes in green areas). On the other hand, the uneven distribution of green and blue zones is also explained by a number of objective reasons, for example, it is almost impossible to perform an eco-friendly renovation of older districts. The participation of NGOs and the academic sector in government environmental policies tends to be through formal channels, even though, according to experts, sometimes these agents fight against the authorities and businesses for the preservation of green zones, which yields results. The economy remains to be of higher priority than the environment with regard to the real estate development of green and blue zones; as a rule, it is not beneficial for businesses to participate in urban greening, though when they do, medium-sized businesses are usually involved. As for the population, the majority (57%) notice positive changes associated with urban greening that have happened over the past five years. Green zones are in demand (for example, in Moscow, the visitor attendance at parks in the summertime increased almost fourfold over the period of 5 years), but for about 30% of the population the parks are still inaccessible by foot. Blue zones are also considered to be popular recreational sites among the population, as almost half of Muscovites (47.9%) and 40% of Kazan citizens say that sometimes they spend time near water bodies, such as rivers, channels, ponds, and lakes in their cities. However, the citizens only give the score of 3.3 out of 5 for the quality and appearance of such water bodies, and 42.7% of the citizens of Moscow and Kazan do not think that the condition of water bodies has changed over the past five years. An expert survey also showed that, for example, in Moscow, the issue of cleaning water bodies has been barely addressed over the past 20 years.

Policy Outcomes

Including a larger number of stakeholders into the process of decision-making concerning the restoration or creation of green and blue zones and the filling up of water bodies; giving priority to environmental interests over economic ones when it comes to building facilities on the territory of green and blue zones; promoting careful attitudes to the urban environment among the population and representatives of the business industry; and introducing restrictions/bans on dumping industrial waste into water bodies. It is necessary to provide the regular cleaning of blue zones. The greening and beautification of yards, small parks, and flower gardens should also be included into the agenda for the population to have green zones within a walking distance.

ENVIRONMENTAL GOVERNANCE AND POLITICS

According to international ratings, the current environmental policy of Russia is becoming less effective in preventing and resolving environmental issues.

However, in the experts' opinion, the situation is steadily improving in the cities included in the research as strategic documents have been accepted, large-scale urban greening and beautification programs developed, environmental and digital innovations implemented, and the environmental agenda is gaining visibility, etc. At the same time, the changes are often associated with the image-building aspects of ecology, such as the planting of parks, while the resolution of problems associated with treatment facilities, sewage, and rundown infrastructure is postponed. Overall, the goals, essence, and efficacy of the environmental policies in Moscow and Kazan show similarities. Thus, despite the fact that environmental issues are part of the strategic development plans in both cities, in reality, a number of problems arise, such as the ambiguous nature of environmental legislative provisions, lack of interdepartmental interaction of authorized bodies when making and implementing managerial decisions, and an almost complete exclusion of professional environmentalists and public representatives from this process, or their involvement as a pure formality. Even though only a small portion of the citizens of Kazan and Moscow in the survey show their concern for environmental issues to some degree, the public effort in combating waste incineration plants and protecting the green zones should not be overlooked. However, the civil ecological activism did achieve the desired results in the majority of the environmental conflicts.

Policy Recommendations

Improving the efficacy of environmental policies in both cities would require, firstly, the systematization of an approach to solving environmental issues, determining the final circle of responsible parties, and developing a unified strategic line of action and interaction for every possible situation. Secondly, it is important to ensure the openness of authorities to the concerns and propositions voiced by all interested parties, especially by professional environmentalists and the local population. It is important to use intersectional approaches and make sure that poor communities, and representatives of minorities and vulnerable groups be able to participate in the decisions related to urban sustainability, and place bottom-up community initiatives at the center of sustainable governance (Carley, Jenkins, & Smith, 2001). The inclusive approach to ecological governance will be possible only with opening up democratic transparent procedures in decision-making which depends on the political climate and democratic transition in Russia.

The rapidly evolving global epidemiological and socio-economic risks caused by COVID-19 are triggering urban structural changes worldwide, including in Russian cities. The pandemic is causing the development of fundamentally new material-discursive processes and practices of consumption, leisure, employment, production chains, and communications. Opportunities for a circular economy and sharing, green and ethical consumption, local production, and decarbonization of the economy are becoming more and more relevant in the decision-making of different city stakeholders. The processes of deurbanization are actively going on, as the lifestyles of residents in the suburbs of cities become more sustainable in the new conditions. Digitalization is forcibly penetrating all spheres of society, blurring the boundaries between global and local, city and village, creating new unexplored opportunities and risks. Considering all these processes, further research is needed to critically explore our understanding of urban sustainability in Russia in the context of the new socio-economic and epidemiological conditions that generate rapid transformations of the Russian cities.

REFERENCES

Abdrahimova, N. M., & Safarov, A. M. (2018). Monitoring i ohrana atmosfernogo vozduha Respubliki Bashkortostan. [Monitoring of atmospheric air protection in the Republic of Bashkortostan.] In A. I. Vostretsov (Ed.), *Nauka, obrazovanie, innovacii: Aprobaciya rezul'tatov issledovanij* (pp. 45–49). Neftekamsk: Mir nauki.

Al-Zu'bi, M., & Radovic, V. (2018). *SDG11 – sustainable cities and communities: Towards inclusive, safe, and resilient settlements.* Bingley: Emerald Publishing Limited.

Andreenko, T. I., Gabderakhmanova, T. S., Danilova, O. V., Ermolenko, G. V., Ermolenko, B. V., Grooms, Yu. N., & Shakun, V. P. (2015). *Atlas of renewable energy resources in Russia.* Moscow: Mendeleyev University of Chemical Technology of Russia.

Autostat. (2017). Rejting rossijskih gorodov-millionnikov po obespechennosti avtomobilyami. [Rating of Russian cities with a million-plus population in terms of car availability.] Retrieved from https://www.autostat.ru/news/29680/

Bakirey, A. S., & Kharitoshkin, N. V. (2014). Razvitie ustojchivyh gorodskih transportnyh sistem v Rossii. [The development of sustainable urban transport systems in Russia.] *Transport Rossijskoj Federacii. Zhurnal o nauke, Ekonomike, Praktike*, *4*(53), 3–7.

Barinova, V. A., Laitner, S., & Lanshina, T. A. (2016). Prospects for renewable energy development in Russia and the world. *SSRN Electronic Journal.* Retrieved from https://papers.ssrn.com/sol3/papers.cfm?abstract_id=2812577. doi:10.2139/ssrn.2812577

Basheva, O. A. (2017). Rossijskie koncepcii ekologizacii gorodov. [Russian concepts of urban greening.] In A. V. Tikhonov (Ed.), *Rossiya i mir: global'nye vyzovy i strategii sociokul'turnoj modernizacii.* Materialy mezhdunarodnoj nauchno-prakticheskoj konferencii (moskva, 12-13 oktyabrya 2017 g.).

(pp. 726–732). Moscow: Federal Center of theoretical and Applied Sociology of the Russian Academy of Sciences.

Beck, U. (1992). *Risk society: Towards a new modernity*. London: SAGE Publications.

Bennetts, M. (2019, April 24). Putin's garbage challenge. *Politico*. Retrieved from https://www.politico.eu/article/vladimir-putin-garbage-problem-russia-landfills/20/

Bobylev, S. N., & Solovyeva, S. V. (2017). Celi ustojchivogo razvitiya dlya budushchego Rossii. [Sustainable development goals for the future of Russia.] *Studies on Russian Economic Development*, *3*(162), 26–33.

Bobylev, S. N., Kudryavtseva, O. V., & Solovyova, S. V. (2014). Indikatory ustojchivogo razvitiya dlya gorodov. [Sustainable development indicators for cities.] *Economy of Region*, *3*(39), 101–110.

Boykova, M., Ilina, I., & Salazkin, M. (2016). The smart city approach as a response to emerging challenges for urban development. *Foresight and STI Governance*, *10*(3), 65–75. doi:10.17323/1995-459X.2016.3.65.75

Boytsov, S. A., Lukyanov, M. M., Deyev, A. D., Klyashtornyy, V. G., Ivanenko, A. V., Volkova, N. S., & Solovyev, D. V. (2016). Vliyaniye ekologicheskikh faktorov na smertnost' naseleniya g. Moskvy; vozmozhnosti otsenki riskov i prognozirovaniya. [The impact of ecological factors on the mortality of the population of Moscow: The prospects of risks assessments and forecast.] *Russian Cardiological Journal*, *6*(134), 34–40. doi:10.15829/1560-4071-2016-6-34-40

Büdenbender, M., & Zupan, D. (2017). The evolution of neoliberal urbanism in Moscow, 1992–2015. *Antipode*, *49*(2), 294–313. doi:10.1111/anti.12266

Bushuyev, V. V., Makarov, A. A., & Mastepanov, A. M. (2010). *Energetika Rossii. 1920–2020 gg. Tom 2. Energeticheskaya politika na rubezhe vekov.* [*Energy of Russia. 1920–2020 gg. Volume 2. Energy policy at the turn of the century.*] Moscow: Energiya.

Bushuyev, V. V. (2014). *Energiya i sud'ba Rossii.* [*Energy and the fate of Russia.*] Moscow: Energiya.

Caprotti, F., & Yu, L. (2018). *Sustainable cities in Asia*. London: Routledge.

Caprotti, F. (2014). Eco-urbanism and the eco-city, or, denying the right to the city? *Antipode*, *46*(5), 1285–1303. doi:10.1111/anti.12087

Carley, M., Jenkins, P., & Smith, H. (2001). *Urban development and civil society: The role of communities in sustainable cities*. London: Earthscan.

Chistaya Rossiya: kak ekologiya stala zadachej №1. [Pure Russia: How ecology has become the #1 challenge.] (2019, December 17). *Gazetaru*. Retrieved from https://www.gazeta.ru/business/2019/12/17/12871220.shtml

Cohen, S. (2017). *The sustainable city*. New York, NY: Columbia University Press.

Da Cruz, N. F., Rode, P., & McQuarrie, M. (2019). New urban governance: A review of current themes and future priorities. *Journal of Urban Affairs*, *41*(1), 1–19. doi:10.1080/07352166.2018.1499416

Davies, A. R. (2008). *The geographies of garbage governance: Interventions, interactions, and outcomes*. Farnham: Ashgate Publishing.

Demidova, A., & Novopashina, N. (2017, August 3). Iz-za programmy 'Moya ulitsa' sokratilos' chislo posetiteley kafe stolitsy. [Due to the my street program, the number of visitors to the capital's cafe has decreased.] *RBC*. Retrieved from https://www.rbc.ru/business/03/08/2017/5981d8fb9a794775e5222e7c

Diani, M. (2003). 'Leaders' or brokers? Positions and influence in social movement networks. In M. Diani & D. McAdam (Eds.), *Social movements and networks: Relational approaches to collective action* (pp. 105–122). Oxford: Oxford University Press. doi:10.1093/0199251789.003.0005. Retrieved from https://www.researchgate.net/publication/285766920

Dolya energoresursov v rossijskom eksporte vyrosla do 70% v yanvare – FTS. [The share of energy in Russian exports rose to 70% in January.] (2017, March 13). *Vedomosti*. Retrieved from https://www.vedomosti.ru/economics/news/2017/03/13/680934-dolya-energoresursov

Domofond.ru. (2018). Rejting ekologicheskogo blagopoluchiya v 150 gorodah Rossii. [Rating of environmental well-being in 150 Russian cities.] Retrieved from https://www.domofond.ru/statya/reyting_ekologicheskogo_blagopoluchiya_v_150_gorodah_rossii/7337

Dronin, N., & Kirilenko, A. (2011). Climate change, food stress, and security in Russia. *Regional Environmental Change*, *11*, 167–178. doi:10.1007/s10113-010-0165-x

Durnitsyna, I. (2013, October 2). 'Umnyj' gorod 'smart siti Kazan' zalozhili v Tatarstane. [Smart' city 'smart city Kazan' was founded in Tatarstan.] *RIA*. Retrieved from https://ria.ru/20131002/967355874.html

Efremenko, D. V., Yanitsky, O. N., & Ermolaeva, P. O. (2019). O sociobiotekhnicheskih sistemah. [About sociobiotechnical systems.] *Voprosy Filosofii*, *5*, 138–147. doi:10.31857/S004287440005064-5

Ekologicheskij rejting rossijskih gorodov 2017: Spisok. [Environmental rating of Russian cities 2017: List.] (2017). Retrieved from https://augustnews.ru/ekologicheskij-rejting-rossijskih-gorodov-2017-spisok/

Ekologiya malogo goroda. [*Ecology of a small city*.] (1981). Pushchino: NCBI AN SSSR.

Elansky, N. F., Shilkin, A. V., Ponomarev, N. A., Semutnikova, E. G., & Zakharova, P. V. (2020). Weekly patterns and weekend effects of air pollution in the Moscow megacity. *Atmospheric Environment*, *224*, 117–303. doi: 10.1016/j.atmosenv.2020.117303

Energy Research Institute of the Russian Academy of Sciences, Analytical Center for the Government of the Russian Federation. (2014). Prognoz razvitiya energetiki mira i Rossii do 2040 goda. [Forecast of the development of energy in the world and Russia until 2040.] Retrieved from https://ac.gov.ru/archive/files/publication/a/2194.pdf

Ermolaeva, P. O., & Ermolaeva, Y. V. (2019). Critical analysis of foreign theories of environmental behavior. *Monitoring of Public Opinion: Economic and Social Changes*, *4*, 323–346. doi:10.14515/monitoring.2019.4.16

Ermolaeva, P. O., Yanitsky, O. N., Basheva, O. A., Ermolaeva, Y. V., & Kuznetsova, I. B. (2019). Social and environmental 'sustainability through changes' of Russian mega-cities: The search for theoretical and methodological approaches. *Monitoring of Public Opinion: Economic and Social Changes*, 2(150), 80–94. doi:10.14515/monitoring.2019.2.04

Ermolaeva, P., Ermolaeva, Y., Kuznetsova, I., Basheva, O., & Korunova, V. (2020). Environmental issues in Russian cities: Towards the understanding of regional and national mass media discourse. *Russian Journal of Communication*, *12*(1), 48–65. doi:10.1080/19409419.2020.1729464

Ermolaeva, P. O. (2014). Citizen (dis)engagement during assessment of sports mega-events: The case of the 2013 Universiade in Kazan, Russia. *Impact Assessment and Project Appraisal*, *32*, 66–71. doi:10.1080/14615517.2014.871810

Ermolaeva, Y. (2015). The culture of waste and social sciences: Searching for a holistic approach. In V. A. Mansurov (Ed.), *Differences, inequalities and sociological imagination: View from Russia* (pp. 340–379). Moscow; Prague: RSS.

Ermolaeva, Y. (2018). Problems of institutionalization of waste management in Russia. *Amazonia Investiga*, *7*(12), 261–266.

Ermolaeva, Y. V. (2019a). Problems of modernization of the waste management sector in Russia: Expert opinions. *Revista Tecnologia e Sociedade*, *15*(35), 56–77. doi:10.3895/rts.v15n35.8502

Ermolaeva, Y. V. (2019b). Zero-waste megapolisy v Rossii: Realizaciya effektivnoj skhemy upravleniya othodami v Rossii po dannym ekspertnogo oprosa na primere moskvy i Kazani. [Zero-waste megacities in Russia: Implementation of an effective waste management scheme in Russia according to an expert survey on the example of moscow and Kazan]. Research result. *Sociology and Management*, *5*(1), 96–108. doi:10.18413/2408-9338-2019-5-1-0-8

Ermolenko, G. V., Proskuryakova, L. N., & Ermolenko, B. V. (2017). Switching to renewables: What will Russia gain? *Foresight*, *19*(5), 528–540. doi:10.1108/FS-01-2017-0002

European Environment Agency. (2013). *Managing municipal solid waste – a review of achievements in 32 European countries: Report (No. 2)*. Luxembourg: Publications Office of the European Union.

Evans, B., Joas, M., Sundback, S., & Theobald, K. (2006). Governing local sustainability. *Journal of Environmental Planning and Management*, *49*(6), 849–867. doi:10.1080/09640560600946875

Evans, A. (2012). Protests and civil society in Russia: The struggle for the Khimki forest. *Communist and Post-communist Studies*, *45*(3–4), 233–242. doi:10.1016/j.postcomstud.2012.06.002

Federal'nyj zakon ob othodah proizvodstva i potrebleniya. (s izmeneniyami na 7 aprelya 2020 goda) (redakciya, dejstvuyushchaya s 14 iyunya 2020 goda). [Federal law about production and consumption waste (as amended on April 7, 2020) (version effective from June 14, 2020).] (2020). Retrieved from http://docs.cntd.ru/document/901711591

Fedorova, N. (2019, December 11). Urbanisty nazvali samye komfortnye i dostupnye dlya zhizni goroda Rossii. [Urbanists named the most comfortable and affordable cities in Russia.] *RBC*. Retrieved from https://www.rbc.ru/business/11/12/2019/5def5b2b9a79472338f48894

Finexpertiza. (2020). Rost v poltora raza: v RF pobit rekord po kolichestvu sluchayev vysokogo zagryazneniya vozdukha. [One and a half times growth: In Russia a record for the number of cases of high air pollution.] Retrieved from https://finexpertiza.ru/press-service/researches/2020/vysok-zagryaznenie-vozdukha/

Gentil, E. C., Damgaard, A., Hauschield, M., Finnveden, G., Eriksson, O., Thorneloe, S., & Christensen, T. H. (2010). Models for waste life cycle assessment: Review of technical assumption. *Waste Management*, *30*, 2636–2648.

Gimalova, R. (2018, June 28). 'Poshli von!' Kak ne sostoyalis' obshchestvennyye slushaniya po MSZ v Osinovo. ['Get out!' How the public hearings on the MRZ in Osinovo did not take place.] *Idelreal*. Retrieved from https://www.idelreal.org/a/29326146.html

Glava Minprirody predlozhil vvesti besplatnye parkovki dlya elektromobilej. [The head of the Ministry of Natural Resources proposed to introduce free parking for electric vehicles.] (2017, December 6). *Kommersant*. Retrieved from https://www.kommersant.ru/doc/3488165

Glubina ozera Kiovo v Lobne uvelichilas' na 15 santimetrov. [The depth of lake Kiovo in Lobna increased by 15 centimeters.] (2017, October 4). *RIAMO*. Retrieved from https://riamo.ru/article/241669/glubina-ozera-kiovo-v-lobne-uvelichilas-na-15-santimetrov.xl

Golubchikov, O., Badyina, A., & Makhrova, A. (2014). The hybrid spatialities of transition: Capitalism, legacy and uneven urban economic restructuring. *Urban Studies*, *51*(4), 617–633. doi:10.1177/0042098013493022

Golubchikov, O. (2017). The post-socialist city: Insights from the spaces of radical societal change. In J. R. Short (Ed.), *A research agenda for cities* (pp. 266–280). Cheltenham: Edward Elgar Publishing. doi: 10.4337/9781785363429.00030

Gonzalez, C. (2013). Environmental justice and international environmental law. In A. I. Shawkat, M. J. Bhuiyan, T. Chowdhury, & E. Techera (Eds.), *Routledge handbook of international environmental law* (pp. 77–97). London: Routledge.

Gosudarstvennyy doklad 'O sostoyanii i ob okhrane okruzhayushchey sredy Rossiyskoy Federatsii v 2016 godu'. [State report 'On the state and environmental protection of the Russian Federation in 2016'.] (2017). Retrieved from http://www.mnr.gov.ru/upload/medialibrary/49b/1-73.pdf

Gosudarstvennyy doklad 'O sostoyanii sanitarno-epidemiologicheskogo blagopoluchiya naseleniya v Rossiyskoy Federatsii v 2017 godu'. [State report 'On the state of sanitary and epidemiological welfare of the population in the Russian Federation in 2017'.] (2018). Retrieved from https://ohranatruda.ru/upload/iblock/c7b/O-sostoyanii-sanitarno_epidemiologicheskogo-blagopoluchiya-naseleniya-v-RF-v-2017-godu.pdf

Greenpeace.ru. (2019). Greenpeace trebuyet razobrat'sya s oslableniyem normativov po formal'degidu i drugim opasnym veshchestvam. [Greenpeace demands weakening Formaldehyde and other hazardous substances.] Retrieved from https://greenpeace.ru/news/2019/02/18/greenpeace-trebuet-razobratsja-s-oslableniem-normativov-po-formaldegidu-i-drugim-opasnym-veshhestvam/?fbclid=IwAR3dbeGexxqvQSPh9Pfk10WnCU6FfiOF30ovRuSGpHQqS4PEqswpIqa1IF8

Greenpeace.ru. (2020). V Moskve i v Podmoskov'ye proshla seriya odinochnykh piketov protiv zagryazneniya vozdukha. [A series of single pickets against air pollution took place in Moscow and the Moscow region.] Retrieved from https://greenpeace.ru/news/2020/02/14/v-moskve-i-v-podmoskove-proshla-serija-odinochnyh-piketov-protiv-zagrjaznenija-vozduha/

Gref: neftyanoy vek v mire zakonchilsya. [Gref: The world's oil age is over.] (2020, March 2). *RIA*. Retrieved from https://ria.ru/20160115/1360068170.html

Grigoriev, V. A., & Ogorodnikov, I. A. (2001). *Problems of cities' ecologization in the world, Russia and Siberia*. Novosibirsk: The State Public Scientific Technological Library of the Siberian Branch of the Russian Academy of Sciences.

Grigorieva, A. (2019, April 25). Roshchu vyrubit', reku zasypat': Razrabotchiki Genplana vtikhuyu podbirayutsya k Kazanke. [Cut down the grove, fill up the river: The city master plan developers quietly approach the Kazanka river.] *Idelreal*. Retrieved from https://www.idelreal.org/a/29902998.html

Gurieva, L. K., & Dzhioev, A. V. (2016). Sustainable development of the Russian economy. *Science Almanac of Black Sea Region Countries*, *2*(6), 5–8.

Haase, D., Dushkova, D., Haase, A., & Kronenberg, J. (2019). Green infrastructure in post-socialist cities: Evidence and experiences from Eastern Germany, Poland and Russia. In T. Tuvikene, W. Sgibnev, & C. S.

Neugebauer (Eds.), *Post-socialist urban infrastructures* (pp. 105–124). London: Routledge. doi:10.4324/9781351190350-7

Hamman, P., Anquetin, V., & Monicolle, C. (2017). Contemporary meanings of the 'sustainable city': A comparative review of the French- and English-language literature. *Sustainable development*, *25*(4), 336–355. doi:10.1002/sd.1660

Hartig, T., Mitchell, R., de Vries, S., & Frumkin, H. (2014). Nature and health. *Annual Review of Public Health*, *35*, 207–228. doi:10.1146/annurev-publhealth-032013-182443

Henry, L. (2010). *Red to green. Environmental activism in post-Soviet Russia.* Ithaca, NY: Cornell University Press.

IAEA. (2019). Russian federation. Retrieved from https://cnpp.iaea.org/countryprofiles/Russia/Russia.htm

Ilyin, V. I. (2000). *Povedenie potrebitelej.* [*Consumer behavior.*] St. Petersburg: Piter.

Ivannikova, T. (2018, September 20). Velosipednye goroda v Rossii – nesbytochnaya mechta? [Cycling cities in Russia – a pipe dream?] Web log message. Retrieved from https://greenpeace.ru/blogs/2018/09/20/velosipednye-goroda-v-rossii-nesbytochnaja-mechta/

Ivanova, N. A., & Lyubimova, K. A. (2019). O karsheringe v Rossijskoj Federacii. [About carsharing in the Russian Federation.] *Civilistika: Pravo I Process*, *4*, 29–35.

Ivantsova, Y. (2019, September 17). Vladimir Burmatov: Proyekt 'chistyy vozdukh' nakhoditsya pod ugrozoy sryva. [Vladimir Burmatov: The clean air project is in jeopardy.] *Fedpress*. Retrieved from https://fedpress.ru/news/77/ecology/2342786

Javeline, D., & Lindemann-Komarova, S. (2019). Financing Russian civil society. *Europe-Asia Studies*, 72(4), 644–685. doi:10.1080/09668136.2019.1637399

K kontsu 2018 goda doma 94% zhiteley Podmoskov'ya obespechat kachestvennoy pit'yevoy vodoy. [By the end of 2018, 94% of Moscow region residents will be provided with quality drinking water at home.] (2018, July 4). *RIAMO*. Retrieved from https://riamo.ru/article/297959/k-kontsu-2018-goda-doma-94-zhitelej-podmoskovya-obespechat-kachestvennoj-pitevoj-vodoj.xl

Karlenzig, W. (2007). *How green is your city? The SustainLane U.S. City rankings*. Gabriola, BC: New Society Publishers.

Kasimov, N. S. (2014). *Regiony i goroda Rossii: Integral'naya ocenka ekologicheskogo sostoyaniya. [Regions and cities of Russia: Integrated environmental assessment.]* Moscow: IP Filimonov M. V

Kazan activists Urge FIFA chief to save trees from world cup parking lot. (2016, November 8). RFE/RL's Tatar-Bashkir Service. Retrieved from https://www.rferl.org/a/russia-kazan-arena-letter-fifa-infantino/28104242.html

Kazan, V. (2017). Yazykom tsifr. [Language of numbers.] Retrieved from http://www.kznvodokanal.ru/about/open-language/

Khaliy, I. A., & Levchenko, N. V. (2017). Ekologicheskoe soznanie rossiyan na puti k ustojchivomu razvitiyu. [Ecological consciousness of Russians on the way to sustainable development.] In O. V. Aksenova (Ed.), *Asimmetriya zhizni sovremennogo rossijskogo obshchestva: Sootnoshenie tradicij i innovacij* (pp. 60–83). Moscow: Federal Research Sociological Centre of the Russian Academy of Sciences.

Kinossian, N. (2012). 'Urban entrepreneurialism' in the post-socialist city: Government-led urban development projects in Kazan, Russia. *International Planning Studies*, *17*(4), 333–352. doi:10.1080/13563475.2012.726850

Kinossian, N. (2017). State-led metropolisation in Russia. *Urban Research & Practice*, *10*(4), 466–476. doi:10.1080/17535069.2016.1275619

Kirakozian, A. (2016). The determinants of household recycling: Social influence, public policies and environmental preferences. *Applied Economics*, *48*(16), 1481–1503. doi:10.1080/00036846.2015.1102843

Klyuchevye vyvody issledovaniya: Sravnitel'nyj analiz Moskvy otnositel'no drugih megapolisov mira po pokazatelyam gradostroitel'nogo razvitiya territorii gorodov. [Key conclusions of the study: Comparative analysis of Moscow relative to other megacities in the world by indicators of urban development of the territory of cities.] (2017). Retrieved from https://www.mos.ru/upload/documents/oiv/versiya_muf_17.pdf

Klyuev, N. N. (2019). Air quality in Russian cities for 1991–2016. *Regional Research of Russia*, *9*(2), 204–212. doi:10.1134/S2079970519020072

Knie, A., & Scherf, K. (2017). Kak transport v gorode mozhet stat' ustojchivym. [How transport in a city can become sustainable.] In *Ustojchivyj transport v gorodskom prostranstve: Perspektivy iz Germanii, Ukrainy i rossii* (pp. 17–32). Saint Petersburg: Nemecko-russkij obmen. Retrieved from http://

www.rnei.de/wp-content/uploads/2017/05/Ustojchivyj-transport-v-gorodskom-prostranstve.pdf

Kolesnikov, A. (2015, May 16). V Moskve stalo men'she derev'ev. [There are fewer trees in Moscow.] *Izvestia*. Retrieved from https://iz.ru/news/586529#ixzz4HdxaI0Dk

Kolesova, E. (2014). Integral'nyj rejting krupnejshih gorodov Rossii. [Integral rating of the largest cities in Russia.] Retrieved from https://docplayer.ru/28309216-Integralnyy-reyting-krupneyshih-gorodov-rossii.html

Koncepciya dolgosrochnogo social'no-ekonomicheskogo razvitiya Rossijskoj Federacii na period do 2020 goda. [Concept of long-term socio-economic development of the Russian Federation for the period up to 2020]. (2018). Retrieved from http://www.consultant.ru/document/cons_doc_LAW_82134/28c7f9e359e8af09d7244d8033c66928fa27e527/

Koncepciya kompleksnogo blagoustrojstva sistemy obshchestvennyh prostranstv. [The concept for the comprehensive improvement of the public spaces system.] (2018). Retrieved from https://dorogomilovo.mos.ru/presscenter/news/detail/7660899.html

Koncepciya vnedreniya intellektual'nyh cifrovyh tekhnologij v Ul'yanovskoj oblasti 'Umnyj region' na 2017–2030 gody. [Concept of introduction of intelligent digital technologies in the Ulyanovsk region 'Smart region' for 2017–2030.] (2017). Retrieved from http://it-fund73.ru/ulsmartregion/Koncept.php

Kondratieva, T., Vibornova, I., & Ismailova, R. (2013). Otsenka ekologicheskogo sostoyaniya vodoyemov goroda Kazani. [The accessment of ecological conditions of water resources of Kazan city.] *Bulletin of the Technological University*, *16*(3), 151–155.

Kopylov, A. E. (2015). *Ekonomika VIE*. [*Economics of RES*.] Moscow: Gryphon.

Korotkov, P. A., & Trubyanov, A. B. (2014). Ocenka ekologicheskoj effektivnosti krupnyh gorodov v usloviyah bystroj urbanizacii. [Assessment of environmental performance of large cities in the context of rapid Urbanization.] *Polythematic Online Scientific Journal of Kuban State Agrarian University*, *102*, 1072–1098.

Korotkov, P. A., Trubyanov, A. B., Zagainova, E. A., & Nikonorov, K. N. (2015). Analiz ustojchivosti ocenok ekologicheskoj effektivnosti krupnyh gorodov. [Analysis of the sustainability assessments on the ecological efficiency of large cities.] *Fundamental research*, *11*(4), 793–797.

Korppoo, A., Tynkkynen, N., & Hønneland, G. (2015). *Russia and the politics of international environmental regimes: Environmental encounters or foreign policy?* Cheltenham: Edward Elgar Publishing.

Kostomarova, A., & Blake, J. (2009, August 25). Russian renewable energy prepares for a bigger slice of the power pie. *RT*. Retrieved from https://www.rt.com/business/russian-renewable-energy-potential/

Kramer, D., & Tikhonova, I. (2015). Water contamination of Moscow's small rivers with different anthropogenic impacts. In C. A. Brebbia (Ed.), *Water resources Management VIII. Transaction series: WIT transactions on ecology and the environment* (pp. 447–457). Southampton: WIT Press.

Kremlin.ru. (2017). Ukaz Prezidenta Rossijskoj Federacii ot 19.04.2017 g. № 176 O Strategii ekologicheskoj bezopasnosti Rossijskoj Federacii na period do 2025 goda. [Decree of the President of the Russian Federation of 19.04.2017 No. 176 on the strategy of environmental security of the Russian Federation for the period up to 2025.] Retrieved from http://kremlin.ru/acts/bank/41879

Kuznetsova, I. (2013). Social'nye posledstviya sportivnyh megasobytij: Mezhdu stimulom i simulyaciej? Razmyshlyaya ob Universiade 2013 v Kazani. [The social consequences of sport mega-events: Between stimulus and simulation? The 2013 Universiade in Kazan.] *Journal of sociology and social anthropology*, *16*(5), 123–140.

Lough, J. (2011, May 20). Russia's energy diplomacy. Retrieved from https://www.chathamhouse.org/publications/papers/view/171229

Lunden, L. P., Fjaertoft, D., Overland, I., & Prachakova, A. (2013). Gazprom vs. other Russian gas producers: The evolution of the Russian gas sector. *Energy Policy*, *61*, 663–670.

Lyakhovenko, O. I., & Chulkov, D. I. (2017). Osnovnye ekologicheskie problemy rossijskih gorodov i strategiya ih razresheniya. [Main environmental problems of Russian cities and their resolution strategy.] *Russian political science*, *3*, 21–26.

Marchenko, O. V., & Solomin, S. V. (2015). O merah po stimulirovaniyu razvitiya vozobnovlyaemyh istochnikov energii. [On measures to stimulate the development of renewable energy sources.] *Science Time*, *4*(16), 472–477.

Medina, M. (2007). *The world's scavengers: Salvaging for sustainable consumption and production.* Lanham, MD: AltaMira Press.

Medvedeva, L. N., Kozenko, K. Y., & Komarova, O. P. (2015). Perspektivy srednih gorodov v razvitii zelenoj ekonomiki. [Prospects of medium-sized cities in the development of green economy.] *News of the complex of Nizhnevolzhsky Agrarian University: Science and Higher Professional Education*, *4*(40), 214–221.

Meerovich, M. G. (2009). Ideya goroda-sada E. Govarda i sovetskie rabochie poselki-sady. [The idea of the garden city of E. Howard and the Soviet working settlements-gardens.] Vestnik Tomskogo gosudarstvennogo arkhitekturno-stroitel'nogo universiteta. *Journal of Construction and Architecture*, *4*, 46–50.

Merle-Beral, E. (2005). Waking the giant. *Our Planet*, *16*(4), 20–21.

Miafodzyeva, S., & Brandt, N. (2013). Recycling behaviour among householders: Synthesizing determinants via a meta-analysis. *Waste and Biomass Valorization*, *4*, 221–235. doi:10.1007/s12649-012-9144-4

Min ekologii Podmoskov'ya nakazalo vinovnika zagryazneniya reki v Krasnogorske. [The Ministry of ecology of the Moscow region punished the culprit of river pollution in Krasnogorsk.] (2017, October 4). *RIAMO*. Retrieved from https://riamo.ru/article/241652/minekologii-podmoskovya-nakazalo-vinovnika-zagryazneniya-reki-v-krasnogorske.xl

Ministry of Construction, Housing and Utilities of the Russian Federation. (n.d.). Proekt Cifrovizacii gorodskogo hozyajstva 'Umnyj gorod'. [The project of digitalization of urban 'smart city'.] Retrieved from http://www.minstroyrf.ru/trades/gorodskaya-sreda/proekt-tsifrovizatsii-gorodskogo-khozyaystva-umnyy-gorod/

Ministry of Ecology and Natural Resources of the Republic of Tatarstan. (2017). Gosudarstvennyy doklad o sostoyanii prirodnykh resursov i ob okhrane okruzhayushchey sredy Respubliki Tatarstan v 2016 godu. [State report on the state of natural resources and environmental protection of the Republic of Tatarstan in 2016.] Retrieved from http://eco.tatarstan.ru/rus/file/pub/pub_1007315.pdf

Ministry of Ecology and Natural Resources of the Republic of Tatarstan. (2019). Gosudarstvennyy doklad o sostoyanii prirodnykh resursov i ob okhrane okruzhayushchey sredy Respubliki Tatarstan. [State report about the conditions of the natural resources and nature preservation in the republic of Tatarstan.] Retrieved from http://eco.tatarstan.ru/rus/gosdoklad-2018.htm

Ministry of Energy of the Russian Federation. (2016). Prognoz nauchno-tekhnologicheskogo razvitiya otraslej TEK. [Forecast of scientific and technological development of the fuel industries.] Retrieved from https://minenergo.gov.ru/node/6366

Ministry of Energy of the Russian Federation. (2018). Otchet ob itogah realizacii Koncepcii otkrytosti federal'nyh organov ispolnitel'noj vlasti v Ministerstve energetiki Rossijskoj Federacii v 2018 godu. [Report on the results of the implementation of the concept of openness of Federal Executive authorities in the Ministry of energy of the Russian Federation in 2018.] Retrieved from https://minenergo.gov.ru/node/14227

Ministry of Energy of the Russian Federation. (n.d.). Energeticheskaya strategiya Rossii na period do 2035 goda (osnovnye polozheniya). [Russian Energy strategy until 2035 (fundamentals).] Retrieved from https://minenergo.gov.ru/node/1026

Ministry of Natural Resources and Environment of the Russian Federation. (2017a). Ekologicheskij rejting gorodov. [Environmental rating of cities.] Retrieved from http://www.mnr.gov.ru/docs/ekologicheskiy_reyting_gorodov/

Ministry of Natural Resources and Environment of the Russian Federation. (2017b). Po mneniyu 44% oproshennyh VCIOM rossiyan, naibol'shuyu ekologicheskuyu opasnost' predstavlyayut bytovye othody. [According to 44% of Russians polled by VCIOM, household waste is the greatest environmental hazard.] Retrieved from http://www.mnr.gov.ru/press/news/po_mneniyu_44_oproshennykh_vtsiom_rossiyan_naibolshuyu_ekologicheskuyu_opasnost_predstavlyayut_bytov/?sphrase_id=37197

Ministry of Natural Resources and Environment of the Russian Federation. (2018). Gosudarstvennyj doklad 'O sostoyanii i ob ohrane okruzhayushchej sredy Rossijskoj Federacii v 2017 godu'. [State report 'On the state and protection of the environment of the Russian Federation in 2017'.] Retrieved from https://www.mnr.gov.ru/docs/o_sostoyanii_i_ob_okhrane_okruzhayushchey_sredy_rossiyskoy_federatsii/gosudarstvennyy_doklad_o_sostoyanii_i_ob_okhrane_okruzhayushchey_sredy_rossiyskoy_federatsii_v_2017_/

Ministry of Transport of the Russian Federation. (2008). Transportnaya strategiya Rossijskoj Federacii na period do 2030 goda. [Transport strategy of the Russian Federation for the period until 2030.] Retrieved from https://www.mintrans.ru/documents/2/1009

Minprirody planiruet sozdat' goskompaniyu po pererabotke musora. [The Ministry of natural resources plans to create a state company for waste processing.] (2018, October 12). *Kommersant*. Retrieved from https://www.kommersant.ru/doc/3767085.

Mironov, V. (2018, September 26). Gorod dlya budushchego. [City for the future]. *RBC+*. Retrieved from https://plus.rbc.ru/news/5baa686f7a8aa93fea4e7a68

Mitsikas, A., & Aravossis, K. G. (2017). A municipal solid waste management assessment guide for waste management plans and reporting. In *Proceedings of the 6th international conference on environmental management, engineering, planning & economics*. Thessaloniki, Εκδόσεις Γράφημα (pp. 466–475).

Mol, A. P. J. (2009). Environmental deinstitutionalization in Russia. *Journal of Environmental Policy and Planning*, *11*(3), 223–241. doi:10.1080/15239080903033812

Morarjee, R. (2010, November 18). Red to green: Russia begins energy saving. Russia. Retrieved from https://www.rbth.com/articles/2010/11/18/red_to_green_russia_begins_energy_saving05128.html

Moscow Department for Environmental Management and Protection. (n.d). Sostoyaniye vodnykh ob'yektov [The condition of water cites.] Retrieved from http://www.dpioos.ru/eco/ru/water

Moscow Mayor Official website. (2013). Predstavlena pyatiletnyaya programma razvitiya 'Moskva — gorod, udobnyj dlya zhizni'. [The five — year development program 'Moscow-a city convenient for life' is presented'.] Retrieved from https://www.mos.ru/mayor/themes/16299/1154050/

Moscow Mayor Official website. (2019a). Bolee dvuh tretej moskvichej postoyanno pol'zuyutsya obshchestvennym transportom. [More than two-thirds of Muscovites constantly use public transport.] Retrieved from https://www.mos.ru/mayor/themes/2299/5344050/

Moscow Mayor Official website. (2019b). Doklad o sostoyanii okruzhayushchey sredy v gorode Moskve v 2018 godu. [Report on the state of the environment in Moscow in 2018.] Retrived from https://www.mos.ru/eco/documents/doklady/view/227443220/

Murray, R. (2002). *Zero waste*. London: Greenpeace Environmental Trust.

"Musornaya reforma" nachalas' v 69 regionah Rossii. ["Garbage reform" started in 69 regions of Russia.] (2019, January 14). *Interfax*. Retrieved from https://www.interfax.ru/russia/646075

Nabiullina, L. (2019, December 4). Dialogi o Kazanke: 'Ona dolzhna ostat'sya zhivoy rekoy – ne invalidom!' [Dialogues about Kazanka: 'It must to stay an alive river – not a disabled!'.] *Business-Online*. Retrieved from https://www.business-gazeta.ru/article/448605

Newell, J. P., & Henry, L. A. (2017). The state of environmental protection in the Russian Federation: A review of the post-Soviet era. *Eurasian Geography and Economics*, *57*, 779–801. doi:10.1080/15387216.2017.1289851

Nikanorov, A. M., Minina, L. I., Bruzgalo, V. A., Kosmenko, L. S., Kondakova, M. Y., Reshetnyak, O. S., & Danilenko, A. O. (2016). Many-year variations of water pollution and the state of river ecosystems in different latitudinal zones in European Russia. *Water Resources*, *43*(5), 791–802.

Ob obrashchenii s tverdymi kommunal'nymi othodami i vnesenii izmeneniya v postanovlenie Pravitel'stva Rossijskoj Federacii ot 25 avgusta 2008 goda N 641 (s izmeneniyami na 15 dekabrya 2018 goda). [About the treatment of solid municipal waste and modification of the resolution of the Government of the Russian Federation of August 25, 2008 N 641 (with changes on December 15, 2018).] (2018a). Retrieved from http://docs.cntd.ru/document/420382731

Ob utverzhdenii koncepcii razvitiya gorodskogo okruga 'Gorod YUzhno-Sahalinsk' s 2018 po 2030 god putem vnedreniya cifrovyh tekhnologij v osnovnyh sferah municipal'noj deyatel'nosti 'Umnyj YUzhno-Sahalinsk' (s izmeneniyami na 27 iyunya 2019 goda). [About the approval of the concept of development of the city district 'city of Yuzhno-Sakhalinsk' from 2018 to 2030 by introduction of digital technologies in the main areas of municipal activity 'Smart Yuzhno-Sakhalinsk' (with changes on June 27, 2019)]. (2019). Retrieved from http://docs.cntd.ru/document/553166669

Obolensky, E. S. (2019). The economy of Russia's garbage disaster. *Economics*, *1*(39), 30–37.

Oktyabrev, S. (2018, September 10). Novaya zhizn' Lebyazh'ikh ozer: kak vosstanavlivali unikal'nyye vodoyemy Kazani. [New life of Lebyazh'okh lakes: how was restored unique water objects of Kazan.] *Sm News*. Retrieved from https://kazan.sm-news.ru/novaya-zhizn-lebyazhix-ozer-kak-vosstanavlivali-unikalnye-vodoemy-kazani/

Open Data Moscow City Government. (n.d). Parkovyye territorii. [Park territories.] Retrieved from https://data.mos.ru/opendata/1465?pageNumber=78&versionNumber=7&releaseNumber=128

Panchuk, A. A. (2015). Problemy i perspektivy ozeleneniya krupnyh gorodov Rossii: Ekonomicheskie, ekologicheskie i social'nye aspekty (na primere Sankt-

Peterburga). [Problems and prospects of greening large cities in Russia: Economic, environmental and social aspects (on the example of st. Petersburg)]. *Herald of Education and Science Development of the Russian Academy of Natural Sciences*, *19*(2), 48–51.

Paramonova, N. (2020). Komu nuzhen 'Chistyĭ vozdukh'. Mozhet li federal'nyў proyekt izmenit' kachestvo vozdukha v gorodakh Rossii? [Who does need a 'clean air'. Can a federal project change the quality of air in Russian cities?] *Environment & Rights*, *77*, 26–29. Retrieved from https://network.bellona.org/content/uploads/sites/4/2020/05/EiP_77_06-1.pdf

Pellow, D. N. (2002). *Garbage wars: The struggle for environmental justice in Chicago*. Cambridge: MIT Press.

Pickett, S. T. A., Boone, C. G., McGrath, B. P., Cadenasso, M. L., Childers, D. L., Ogden, L. A., & Grove, J. M. (2013). Ecological science and transformation to the sustainable city. *Cities*, *32*(1), 10–20. doi:10.1016/j.cities.2013.02.008

Pochti 760 tysyach rubley shtrafov vypisali posle proverki butilirovannoy vody v Moskve. [Almost 760 thousand rubles of fines were issued after checking bottled water in Moscow.] (2018, August 9). *M24.ru*. Retrieved from https://www.m24.ru/news/bezopasnost/09082018/41692

Podobedova, L., & Kalyukov, E. (2019, December 25). Chemezov ocenil potrebnost' Rossii v musoroszhigatel'nyh zavodah. [Chemezov assessed Russia's need for incineration plants.] *RBC*. Retrieved from https://www.rbc.ru/business/25/12/2019/5e0385549a794707920c810c

Postanovlenie ob utverzhdenii Territorial'noj skhemy v oblasti obrashcheniya s othodami, v tom chisle s tverdym kommunal'nym othodami, Respubliki Tatarstan. [Resolution on approval of the Territorial scheme in the field of waste management, including solid municipal waste, of the Republic of Tatarstan.] (2016). Retrieved from http://pravo.tatarstan.ru/rus/file/npa/2016-10/81845/npa_81846.pdf

Pravitelstvo Sevastopolya. (n.d). Umnyj gorod. [Smart city.] Retrieved from https://sev.gov.ru/goverment/priorities/51710/

Proekt 'Smart siti Kazan' zamorozhen, struktura, razvivavshaya ego, uprazdnena. [The Smart city Kazan project has been frozen, and the structure that developed it has been abolished.] (2015, January 22). *Kazan.MK.ru*. Retrieved from https://kazan.mk.ru/articles/2015/01/22/proekt-smart-siti-kazan-zamorozhen-struktura-razvivavshaya-ego-uprazdnena.html

Progress on household drinking water, sanitation and hygiene 2000–2017. Special focus on inequalities. (2019a). New York, NY: United Nations Children's Fund (UNICEF) and World Health Organization (WHO).

Proyekt musoroszhigatel'nogo zavoda v Osinovo odobrili nemetskiye eksperty. [Osinovo waste incinerator project approved by German experts.] (2020, May 19). *Idelreal*. Retrieved from https://www.idelreal.org/a/30620519.html

Public Opinion Foundation. (2016). Gorozhane o rabote nazemnogo obshchestvennogo transporta. [Citizens on the work of public transport.] Retrieved from http://fom.ru/Obraz-zhizni/12662

Ratner, S. V., & Nizhegorodtsev, R. M. (2017). Analysis of renewable energy projects' implementation in Russia. *Thermal Engineering*, *64*(6), 429–436. doi:10.1134/S0040601517060052

Rejting ekologicheskogo razvitiya gorodov Rossii – 2017. [Rating of environmental development of Russian cities – 2017.] (2017a). Retrieved from http://www.acexpert.ru/analytics/ratings/reyting-ekologicheskogo-razvitiya-gorodov-rossii.html

Rejting ekologicheskogo upravleniya gorodov Rossii – 2015. [Rating of the environmental management of Russian cities – 2015.] (2015). Retrieved from http://volcomsys.ru/userfiles/files/rejting.pdf

Rejting rossijskih gorodov po zagryazneniyu atmosfery v 2012 godu. [Rating of Russian cities by air pollution in 2012.] (2013, August 6). *RIA*. Retrieved from https://ria.ru/infografika/20130806/954525899.html

REN21. (2011). *Renewables 2011 global status report*. Paris: REN21 Secretariat.

Revich, B., & Shaposhnikov, D. (2010). The effects of particulate and ozone pollution on mortality in Moscow, Russia. *Air Quality, Atmosphere & Health*, *3*(2), 117–123. doi:10.1007/s11869-009-0058-7

Revich, B. A., Avaliani, A. S., & Simons, G. (2016). Air pollution and public health in a megalopolis: A case study of moscow. *Economy of Region*, *4*(12), 1069–1078. doi:10.17059/2016–4–9

Richler, J. (2019). International perspectives. *Nature Climate Change*, *9*, 4–6. doi:10.1038/s41558-018-0374-8

Rosatom do 2024 g sozdast za 36 mlrd rub 7 kompleksov pererabotki promothodov 1 i 2 klassa. [Rosatom will create 7 complexes for processing class 1 and 2 waste products for 36 billion rubles by 2024.] (2018, September 12). *Prime*. Retrieved from https://1prime.ru/energy/20180912/829221977.html

Rukov, K. (2018, February 16). Musornyy bunt: Za chto moskve dolzhno byt' stydno. [Garbage riot: For which moscow should be ashamed.] *The Village*. Retrieved from https://www.the-village.ru/village/city/infrastructure/301663-musor-che-s-nim-proihodit#%D0%9A%D1%83%D1%87%D0%B8%D0%BD%D0%BD%D0%BE%D0%BE%D0%BE%D0%BD%D0%BD%D0%BE%D0%BE

Rylova, E. (2018, April 17). Kazgorduma opredelila, kto budet shtrafovat' za parkovku v zelenoy zone. [Kazgorduma has determined who will fine for parking in the green zone.] *RBC Tatarstan*. Retrieved from https://rt.rbc.ru/tatarstan/freenews/5ad60b2a9a794728ef5fa050

Safroshkin, Y. V. (1991). Ekopolis – shans na budushchee. Osnovy koncepcii garmonichnyh nizovyh yacheek rasseleniya noosfery (otchet o poiskovoj NIR). [Ecopolis-a chance for the future. Fundamentals of the concept of harmonious grassroots cells of the noosphere settlement (report on the search research).] Retrieved from http://sumi.ulstu.ru/static/noo/yusafr/ecopolis.pdf

Saginova, O. V., & Zavyalova, N. B. (2018). Velosiped v transportnoj sisteme sovremennogo megapolisa. [Bicycle in the transport system of the modern metropolis.] *Rossiyskoe predprinimatelstvo*, *19*(12), 4143–4158. doi: 10.18334/rp.19.12.39663

Saginova, O. V. (2019). Mezhdunarodnyj opyt razvitiya mobil'nosti v megapolise. [International experience in the development of mobility in a megalopolis.] *ETAP: Economic Theory, Analysis, and Practice*, *1*, 70–81. doi: 10.24411/2071-6435-2019-10069

Sardzhveladze, S. (2018, June 8). Raskhody na 'Moyu ulitsu' za god vyrosli na 5 mlrd rub. [Expenses for 'my street' for the year increased by 5 billion rubles.] *RBC*. Retrieved from https://www.rbc.ru/society/08/06/2018/5b1954509a79475e24996e13

Schübeler, P. (1996). Conceptual framework for municipal solid waste management in low-income countries. In K. Wehrle & J. Christen (Eds.), *UNDP/UNCHS/World Bank/SDC collaborative programme on municipal solid waste management in low-income countries* (pp. 59–70). St. Gallen: SKAT.

Schwartz, S. H. (1977). Normative influences on altruism. *Advances in Experimental Social Psychology*, *10*(1), 221–279. doi:10.1016/s0065-2601(08)60358-5

Semashko, N. (2018, November 21). Teplovoy eksperiment. [Thermal experiment.] *Kommersant*. Retrieved from https://www.kommersant.ru/doc/3787078

Semerkin, S. (2019, April 5). Kazan' vyydet k Volge. [Kazan will move out to Volga.] *Respublika Tatarstan*. Retrieved from http://rt-online.ru/kazan-vyjdet-k-volge/

Serova, I. (2017, November 29). Der"mo vopros: Obitateley elitnykh kottedzhnykh poselkov pod Kazan"yu lishili kanalizatsii. [Another question: Residents of elite cottage settlements near Kazan were deprived of sewerage.] *Evening Kazan*. Retrieved from http://www.evening-kazan.ru/articles/dermo-vopros-obitateley-elitnyh-kottedzhnyh-poselkov-pod-kazanyu-lishili-kanalizacii.html

SGM. (2015). Rejting ustojchivogo razvitiya gorodov RF za 2015 god. [Rating of sustainable development of Russian cities for 2015]. Retrieved from http://www.agencysgm.com/projects/%D0%A0%D0%B5%D0%B9%D1%82%D0%B8%D0%BD%D0%B3%20%D1%83%D1%81%D1%82%D0%BE%D0%B9%D1%87%D0%B8%D0%B2%D0%BE%D0%B3%D0%BE%20%D1%80%D0%B0%D0%B7%D0%B2%D0%B8%D1%82%D0%B8%D1%8F-2015.pdf

Shabanova, M. A. (2019). Razdel'nyj sbor bytovyh othodov v Rossii: Uroven', faktory i potencial vklyucheniya naseleniya. [Separate collection of household waste in Russia: Level, factors and population inclusion potential.] *Universe of Russia*, *3*(28), 88–112. doi:10.17323/1811-038X-2019-28-3-88-112

Shelekhov, A. M. (Ed.). (2002). *Osnovnye polozheniya strategii ustojchivogo razvitiya Rossii.* [*Main provisions of the Russian sustainable development strategy.*] Retrieved from http://www-sbras.nsc.ru/win/sbras/bef/strat.html

Sotnik, O. (2017, November 13). Kazan' za god potratila boleye 1 mlrd rubley na parki i vodoyemy. [Kazan 'spent over 1 billion rubles on parks and ponds in a year.] *RBC Tatarstan*. Retrieved from https://rt.rbc.ru/tatarstan/freenews/5a09593b9a794774121c88f7

Sotsseti: Vladelets kottedzha v CHelnakh s·ekonomil na kanalizatsii, sdelav sliv pryamo v rechku. [Social networks: The owner of a cottage in Chelny saved on sewage by making a drain directly into the river.] (2018, June 26). *Business-Online*. Retrieved from https://www.business-gazeta.ru/article/386765

Stecenko, K. (2016, September 20). Ekologicheskiy ekstrim: kak dayvery i ekologi spasayut reki Podmoskov'ya. [Ecological extream: How divers and ecologists rescue Moscow area rivers.] *RIAMO*. Retrieved from https://riamo.ru/article/162260/ekologicheskij-ekstrim-kak-dajvery-i-ekologi-spasayut-reki-podmoskovya.xl

Stern, P. C. (2000). New environmental theories: Toward a coherent theory of environmentally significant behavior. *Journal of Social Issues*, *56*(3), 407–424. doi:10.1111/0022-4537.00175

Stern, P. C. (2005). Understanding individuals' environmentally significant behavior. *Environmental Law Reporter*, *35*(5), 10785–10790.

Steshenko, A. Y. (2018). Analiz protestnoj aktivnosti mestnogo naseleniya protiv svalok v ekologicheskih. [Analysis of the protest activity of the local population against landfills in the environmental conflicts of the Moscow region.] *Scyth*, *6*(22), 15–20.

Svirin, A. (2019, April 18). V CODD Moskvy zayavili o roste kolichestva lichnyh avto na tret'. [Moscow's data center announced a third increase in the number of personal cars.] *Sm News*. Retrieved from https://sm-news.ru/v-codd-moskvy-zayavili-o-roste-kolichestva-lichnyx-avto-na-tret-1327/

Sychev, P. (2017, October 26). Vlasti Kazani budut razvivat' besplatnyy wifi vo dvorakh. [Kazan authorities will develop 'free wifi in the yards.] *RBC Tatarstan*. Retrieved from https://rt.rbc.ru/tatarstan/freenews/59f18c2e9a7947bf38e69f37

TAdviser. (2020). Moskva – Umnyj gorod. [Moscow – smart city.] Retrieved from https://urlid.ru/by4w

Tafeyeva, E. A., Ivanov, A. V., Titova, A. A., & Akhmetzyanova, I. F. (2015). Monitoring zagryazneniya atmosfernogo vozdukha kak faktora riska zdorov'yu naseleniya Kazani. [Air pollution monitoring as factor of risks of health of the population of Kazan.]. *Hygiene and Sanitation*, *94*(3), 37–40.

Tat'yana Prokof'yeva: 'Kazan' spokoyno mozhet razmestit' i 3 milliona chelovek'. [Tatyana Prokofieva: 'Kazan can easily accommodate 3 million people'.] (2017, December 5). *Business-Online*. Retrieved from https://www.business-gazeta.ru/article/365925

Territorial'naya skhema obrashcheniya s othodami, v tom chisle s tverdymi kommunal'nymi othodami, Moskovskoj oblasti. [Territorial waste management scheme, including the number of municipal solid waste, Moscow region.] (2016a). Retrieved from http://rsbor-msk.ru/wp-content/uploads/2017/07/%D0%9F%D1%80%D0%B8%D0%BB%D0%BE%D0%B6%

D0%B5%D0%BD%D0%B8%D0%B5_%D0%BA_%D0%9F%D0%9F_%D0%9C%D0%9E_%E2%84%96984_47_%D0%BE%D1%82_22.pdf

Tetior, A. N. (2016). *Novaya koncepciya filosofskogo osmysleniya mira i evolyucii zhivoj prirody.* [*A new concept of philosophical understanding of the world and the evolution of living nature.*] Moscow: Akademii Estestvoznaniya.

Tetior, A. N. (2017). New conception of creation of 'zero' ecobuildings and ecocities on base of ecological infrastructure. *European Journal of Natural History*, 5, 22–26.

The Center for Strategic Research "North-West". (2018). *Prioritetnye napravleniya vnedreniya tekhnologij umnogo goroda v rossijskih gorodah: Ekspertno-analiticheskij doklad.* [*Priority directions for implementing smart city technologies in Russian cities: Expert and analytical report.*] The Center for Strategic Research "North-West", Moscow.

Tishchenko, I. (2018, June 14). Koncepciyu 'Umnyj Sankt-Peterburg' predstavili v smol'nom. [The concept of 'smart Saint-Petersburg' presented in Smolny.]. *spbdnevnik.ru*. Retrieved from https://spbdnevnik.ru/news/2018-06-14/kontseptsiyu-umnyy-sanktpeterburg-predstavili-v-smolnom

Trentmann, F. (2007). Citizenship and consumption. *Journal of Consumer Culture*, 7(2), 147–158. doi:10.1177/1469540507077667

Tysiachniouk, M., Tulaeva, S., & Henry, L. A. (2018). Civil society under the law 'on foreign agents': NGO strategies and network transformation. *Europe-Asia Studies*, *70*(4), 615–637. doi:10.1080/09668136.2018.1463512

Ulanova, O. V., & Tulohonova, A. V. (2013). *Ocenka zhiznennogo cikla integrirovannyh sistem upravleniya othodami.* [*Life cycle assessment of integrated waste management systems.*] Moscow: Akademiya Estestvoznaniya.

'Umnyj region' - SMART REGION (2018). Koncepciya postroeniya na territorii Sverdlovskoj oblasti. ['Smart region' - SMART REGION. Concept of building on the territory of the Sverdlovsk region.] Retrieved from http://www.acexpert.ru/analytics/projects/umniy-region–smart-region-koncepciya-postroeniya-.html

UN-Habitat-Nairobi, KE, United Nations Human Settlements Programme, UNEP-Nairobi, KE. (1999). *Institutionalising the environmental planning and management (EPM) process: The sustainable cities programme (SCP).* Source book series (Vol. 5). Nairobi: UN-Habitat, United Nations Centre for Human Settlements.

United Nations. (2015a). Global waste management outlook. Retrieved from https://www.uncclearn.org/sites/default/files/inventory/unep23092015.pdf

United Nations. (2015b). Paris agreement. Retrieved from https://unfccc.int/files/essential_background/convention/application/pdf/english_paris_agreement.pdf

V dvukh gorodakh RT zafiksirovano zagryazneniye vozdukha, prevyshayushcheye predel'no dopustimuyu kontsentratsiyu. [In two cities of the Republic of Tatarstan, air pollution is recorded exceeding the maximum permissible concentration.] (2019, March 22). *Business-Online*. Retrieved from https://www.business-gazeta.ru/news/417949

V Kazani proekt formirovaniya komfortnoj sredy obeshchali soglasovyvat' s gorozhanami. [In Kazan, the project of creating a comfortable environment promised to coordinate with citizens.] (2017, October 26). *Business-Online*. Retrieved from https://www.business-gazeta.ru/news/361942

V Menzelinskom rayone stochnyye vody zagryaznili reku Elkhovku. [In the Menzelinsky district, sewage polluted the Elkhovka river.] (2018, June 21). *Business-Online*. Retrieved from https://www.business-gazeta.ru/article/386158

V Moskve na blagoustroyennykh ulitsakh vysadili okolo trekh tysyach derev'yev. [About three thousand trees were planted in landscaped streets in Moscow.] (2017, November 21). *RIA*. Retrieved from https://ria.ru/20171121/1509203896.html

V Moskve priostanovlena rabota asfal'tobetonnogo zavoda iz-za vrednykh vybrosov. [In Moscow, the work of an asphalt concrete plant was suspended due to harmful emissions.] (2018, August 27). *Vedomosti*. Retrieved from https://www.vedomosti.ru/business/news/2018/08/27/779072-asfaltobetonnogo-zavoda

V Odintsovskom rayone oshtrafovali predpriyatiye, ekspluatiruyushcheye ochistnyye sooruzheniya. [In the Odintsovo district, a company operating treatment facilities was fined.] (2017, October 4). *RIAMO*. Retrieved from https://riamo.ru/article/241626/v-odintsovskom-rajone-oshtrafovali-predpriyatie-ekspluatiruyuschee-ochistnye-sooruzheniya.xl

V parke 850-letiya Moskvy zavershayetsya ustroystvo sportivnykh ploshchadok. [In the park of the 850th anniversary of Moscow, the completion of sports facilities.] (2018, September 14). *RIA*. Retrieved from https://realty.ria.ru/20180914/1528553579.html

V Rossii sostavlen rejting privlekatel'nosti gorodskoj sredy prozhivaniya. [In Russia, a rating of attractiveness of the urban living environment has been compiled.] (2013, December 18). *RBC*. Retrieved from http://realty.rbc.ru/news/577d25fb9a7947a78ce9235c

Van Wee, B., & Handy, S. (2016). Key research themes on urban space, scale, and sustainable urban mobility. *International Journal of Sustainable Transportation*, *10*(1), 18–24. doi:10.1080/15568318.2013.820998

Varol, T. (2013). *The Russian foreign energy policy*. Kocani: EGALITE.

'Vazhny tekhnologicheskie kompetencii'. ['Technological competence is important'.] (2017, May 15). *Kommersant*. Retrieved from https://www.kommersant.ru/doc/3292668

VCIOM: bol'she poloviny rossiyan tshchatel'no sledyat za potrebleniem energoresursov. [VTSIOM: More than half of Russians carefully monitor energy consumption.] (2019, October 8). *TASS*. Retrieved from https://tass.ru/obschestvo/6973650

VCIOM: Za energopotrebleniem ne sledit kazhdyj desyatyj rossiyanin. [VTSIOM: Every tenth Russian does not monitor energy consumption.] (2019, March 29). *Interessant*. Retrieved from https://www.interessant.ru/people/vtsiom-za-raskhodom-enierg

Vernadsky, V. I. (1991). *Nauchnaya mysl' kak planetnoe yavlenie*. [*Scientific thought as a planetary phenomenon*.] Moscow: Nauka.

Von Weizsäcker, E. U., Hargrouz, K., & Smith, M. (2013). *Faktor 5. Formula ustojchivogo rosta*. [*Factor 5. The formula for sustainable growth*.] Moscow: Art Press.

Vuchic, V. R. (1999). *Transportation for livable cities*. London: Routledge.

WaterMap. (2018). Vodnaya karta Rossii. [Water map of Russia.] Retrieved from http://watermap.ru/moscow

Williams, A. M. (1998). Therapeutic landscapes in holistic medicine. *Social Science & Medicine*, *46*(9), 1193–1203. doi:10.1016/S0277-9536(97)10048-X

Williams, A. M. (Ed.). (2017). *Therapeutic landscapes*. Hoboken, NJ: John Wiley & Sons. doi:10.1002/9781118786352.wbieg0138

Wolch, J. R., Byrne, J., & Newell, J. P. (2014). Urban green space, public health, and environmental justice: The challenge of making cities 'just green enough'. *Landscape and Urban Planning*, *125*, 234–244. doi:10.1016/j.landurbplan.2014.01.017

World Health Organization Regional Office for Europe. (2017). Gorodskiye zelenyye zony: kratkoye rukovodstvo k deystviyu. [Urban green zones: A quick guide to action.] Retrieved from http://www.euro.who.int/__data/assets/pdf_file/0020/342290/Urban-Green-Spaces_RUS_WHO_web.pdf

World Health Organization. (2009). Global health risks: Mortality and burden of disease attributable to selected major risks. Retrieved from https://apps.who.int/iris/handle/10665/44203

Yanitsky, O., & Usacheva, O. (2017). History of the 'green city' in Russia. *Journal of History Culture and Art Research*, *6*(6), 125–131. doi:10.7596/taksad.v6i6.1330

Yanitsky, O. N. (2012). From nature protection to politics: The Russian environmental movement 1960–2010. *Environmental Politics*, *21*(6), 922–940. doi:10.1080/09644016.2012.724216

Yanitsky, O. N. (2018a). On transition to postmodernity and the role of an 'ideal city' modeling. *International Journal of Political Science*, *4*(3), 49–56. doi:10.20431/2454-9452.0403007

Yanitsky, O. N. (2018b). Rossijskie megapolisy v usloviyah global'nyh social'no-ekologicheskih vyzovov. [Russian megacities in the context of global social and environmental challenges.] *Obshchestvennye Nauki I Sovremennost*, *1*, 5–16.

Yanitsky, O. N. (2018c). The development of the Russian environmental movement in the beginning of XXI century. *International Journal of Humanities Social Sciences and Education (IJHSSE)*, *5*(6), 23–31. doi: 10.20431/2349-0381.0506004

Yukhnovskaya, O. (2018, October 16). 'Narod imeet pravo znat''!: Grinpis issledoval vozduh v Kazani. ['People has a right to know!: Greanpeace has studied the air in Kazan.] *Evening Kazan*. Retrieved from http://www.evening-kazan.ru/articles/narod-imeet-pravo-znat-grinpis-issledoval-vozduh-v-kazani.html

Zelenyye nasazhdeniya v moskve: bol'she naroda, men'she kisloroda. [Green spaces in moscow: More people, less oxygen.] (2015, May 8). *Ecoportal*. Retrieved from http://ecoportal.su/news.php?id=82963

Zupan, D., & Büdenbender, M. (2019). Moscow urban development: Neoliberal urbanism and green infrastructures. In T. Tuvikene, W. Sgibnev, & C. S. Neugebauer (Eds.), *Post-socialist urban infrastructures* (pp. 125–141). London: Routledge.

INDEX

Adjusted net savings index (ANS index), 13–14
Air pollution
  attitudes toward air pollution among population and protests against waste incineration plants, 22–24
  in Russia, 20–21
Air quality
  contested monitoring, factors of pollution and policies, 20–22
  current condition and trends in development of Russian water supply system, 24–27
  monitoring in Russia, 19
  policy recommendations, 99
  special aspects of Russian policies aimed at solving water quality issues, 27–30
  and water quality, 98–99
Akademicheskiy microdistrict in Yekaterinburg, 9
Almetyevsk city, 39–40

Beautification principles, 72–73
Biopositivity, 7
Biotic City, 7
Blue zones, 71–72, 80, 103–104
  condition and major problems, 72–82
  policy outcomes, 104
Brown economy models, media discourse on, 49–51
Business, 61
Business-Online (e-journals), 2–3

Car sharing institution in Russia, 41–42
Centralized waste management, 58
Citizens' attitudes and practices, 37–42
City sustainability index, 14
Civic engagement in environmental governance, 91–95
"Clean Air" federal program, 21
"Compact City", 5
Conservation of energy, 48
Contextual theory, 12

Deecologization, 84–85
Desk research, 2
"Development of comfortable urban environment in 2018–2022" municipal program, 75
Domestic waste, 57–58
"Domofond. ru" analysts, 15
Double transition process, 1

E-journals, 2–3
Eco-transport, 35
"Ecocity", 5
Ecological Doctrine of the Russian Federation, 7–8
Ecological policy in Russian cities, 83–85
Ecologization of human activity, 7
Economic regulation of RES, 49
Ecopolis, 6–7
Electric buses, 36
Electric vehicles, 35

Emissions per unit of energy generated, 46
Energy efficiency, 46
  in cities, 48
  and consumption, 100–102
  policy recommendations, 101–102
Energy intensity, 46
Energy market economics in Russia, 45
Energy priorities of Russian cities, 46
Energy saving practices among Russians, 52–55
"Environmental Cities of the Future" project, 7
Environmental governance and politics, 104–106
  civic engagement in environmental governance, 91–95
  ecological policy in Russian cities, 83–85
  in Moscow and Kazan via prism of professionals' opinions, 85–91
  policy recommendations, 105–106
Environmental inequality, 68–70
Environmental justice concept, 11–12
Environmental Performance Index, 97
Environmental policy, 84–85
"Environmental rating of Russian cities", 16
Environmental Security Strategy of Russian Federation, 8
Environmentalists, 90
Expert
  assessment of developing sustainable energy in Russia, 47–49
  interviews, 67
Export-oriented geopolitics, 50–51

Federal Antimonopoly Service (FAS), 49–50
Federal Environmental Protection Law, 7–8
Federal waste management system, 58
"Foreign agents" law, 85

"Garden City", 5–6
Gas-fueled cars, 34–35
Good governance, 83
"Green City", 5
Green economy models, media discourse on, 49–51
Green energy, 47–48
Green Patrol, 16–17
Green zones, 71–72, 76–77, 103–104
  condition and major problems, 72–82
  policy outcomes, 104
Greenhouse gas emissions, 31
"Greening" in Russia's cities, 1–2
Greenpeace, 20–21, 73

Incineration plants, 60
Index of Sustainable Development of Cities in Russian Federation, 97
Industrial waste, 57–58
Innopolis satellite towns in Kazan, 9
Integral Index of City Sustainability, 13–14

Kazan, 74
  air polluted regions, 20, 26–27
  greening and beautification agenda, 75
  policy of Kazan authorities, 30

Landfills, 59–60
"Low Carbon City", 5

M24. ru, RIAMO (e-journals), 2–3
"Map of Destroyed Roads" project, 75

Mass media discourse analysis, 2–3
Mathematical models, 1–2
Media discourse on "brown" and "green" economy models, 49–51
Mixed methods approach, 3
Moscow
  air polluted regions, 20
  quality of water supply in, 24
Mospravda. ru (e-journals), 2–3
Motor vehicles, 31
"My Street" beautification program ("*Moya Ulitsa*"), 74

National Environmental Action Plan of Russian Federation, 7–8
Natural gas vehicle fuel (NGV fuel), 35
"Nature and Recreation Complex", 74
Newspapers, 2–3
Non-governmental organizations (NGOs), 3
Nonprofit organizations (NPOs), 28
Noosphere, 6

Optimistic forecast, 48
Osinovo village, 22

Pessimistic
  forecast, 48
  scenario, 63
Positive (constructive) scenario, 64
Pro-environmental behavior theories, heuristic possibilities of, 12
Professional divers, 81
Professional environmentalists from Kazan, 90–91
Project of Moscow Socioeconomic Development Strategy, 84
Public engagement, 68–70
Public hearings, 91
Public polls, 67
Public transport(ation), 15–16, 33–34, 38
Purposive sampling, 3
Pyat' Gigavatt program, 46

RBK, 75
Reclamation resources, 58
Recycled paper market, 61
Recycling, 58
Regeneration, 58
Renewable energy
  in Russia, 46–47
  sources, 36, 47
Renewables, 48–49
Republic of Tatarstan, 74
RIAMO, 28–29
Rosatom State Corporation, 63
Russia
  energy market economics in, 45
  modern waste management system in, 57–65
  sustainable transport and mobility in, 31–37
Russian cities, 1
Russian energy system, 43
  energy and water saving practices among Russians, 52–55
  expert assessment of developing sustainable energy in Russia, 47–49
  features and development prospects, 43–45
  media discourse on "brown" and "green" economy models, 49–51
  traditional and renewable energies in Russia, 46–47
Russian Environmental Operator, 58–59
Russian environmental policy, 83–84
Russian Geographical Society, 14
Russian mega-cities, 10

Russian water supply system, current condition and trends in development of, 24–27
Russians' waste management practices, 65–68

Skolkovo science city in Moscow, 9
SMART City, 9
"Smart Sustainable City", 5
Socio-biotechnical systems (SBT systems), 10
Stagnation scenario, 63
Stakeholders, 48–49
Sustainability of city, 32
Sustainable cities, 5, 9, 97
Sustainable Cities Program, 5
Sustainable mobility, 37–42
Sustainable transport and mobility, 31, 100
  policy recommendations, 100
  in Russia, 31–37
Sustainable transport systems, 33
  creation, 31–32
  requirements, 34
Sustainable urban development, 5
  principles, 7
Sustainable urban development, principles of, 98
Systemic enterprises, 46

Tatar-inform (e-journals), 2–3
Traditional energies in Russia, 46–47
Transportation for livable cities, 31–32

Urban density, 46
Urban governance, 83
Urban greening, 72–73
Urban policy, 29
Urban sustainability, 12
«Urbanika» Institute, 15

Vechernya Kazan (e-journals), 2–3
Vechernyaya Kazan, 29
Vehicle emissions, 21–22
Volunteers, 81

Waste collapse, 61
Waste incineration plants, attitudes toward air pollution among population and protests against, 22–24
Waste management, 102–103
  environmental inequality, waste-related conflicts, and public engagement, 68–70
  modern waste management system in Russia, 57–65
  policy recommendations, 102–103
  Russians' waste management practices, 65–68
Waste-related conflicts, 68–70
Water
  saving practices among Russians, 52–55
  supply networks, 29–30
WIPs, 61
Workplaces, 62
World Health Organization (WHO), 71

Yadrovo open-air landfill, 69
Yuzhny satellite town in Saint Petersburg, 9

Zero-waste
  concept, 11
  economy in Russian cities, 58–59
  policy, 57